Reader's

"Money's Big Secret will make you question everything you've ever bought."

"This is not an ordinary book about money: Tom Church delivers on his word."

"I can't believe he starved himself for a week. You have to read it for that reason alone!"

"Fantastic. No one has ever explained money like this before."

"Most money books say, 'save this, save that'. Not here. Money's Big Secret is best I've read."

"Writing about the real nature of money isn't easy. Tom makes it sound like a nursery rhyme."

"No nonsense, practical advice everyone can apply. Tom is obviously mad and I love it."

"Combine Martin Lewis with David Attenborough and you get Tom Church. Riveting."

"If you're stuck in debt, read this book. If you don't understand money, read this book. If you can't save money, read this book. Just read it."

"Tom shares the fundamentals of money and explains how this determines what we do with it. He then provides practical steps to take advantage of money's secret nature."

"Wonderfully written, money is fun to talk about again."

"The single best thing since sliced bread."

"Money's Big Secret will help a lot of people."

"Really good. If you're ever going to read a personal finance book, this is the one to choose."

"This is a short book for a reason: Tom tells you what you need to know and nothing more. An excellent read."

"You'll wish you had read this ten years ago."

Money's Big Secret

TOM CHURCH

Church & Company

Published by Church & Company

Copyright © Church & Company 2016

This book is sold subject to the condition that it shall not, by way of trade or otherwise, be lent, resold, hired out, or otherwise circulated without the publisher's prior consent in any form of binding or cover other than that in which it is published and without a similar condition including being imposed on the subsequent purchaser.

First published in the United Kingdom in 2016 by Church & Company, London.

More information can be found at tomchurch.co.uk

Church & Company is the trading name of Church & Company (Consultancy) Ltd.
Company number 8840194

PREFACE

"I'm writing a book," said Tom.
"What about?" I asked.
"It's a book on money."
"Hasn't that been done before?"
"Not like this, this will be a *classic*."

If anyone else had told me this I would have rolled up my eyes. However, having known Tom for years I knew he was serious.

Tom has a contrarian way of thinking that's both ridiculous and genius.

I remember when we first met in a bar by St. Paul's Cathedral in London. He was still at University and wanted to learn what makes some businesses more successful than others. Whereas most students do internships and work experience, Tom said, "How does that help? You only learn about one business at a time and can't compare them."

Instead, he created a business networking group which grew into London's biggest. In just over a year he had over two thousand members and hundreds came every month. It's here that I met him. I had just launched my website, LatestFreeStuff.co.uk, and Tom discussed it with me for hours that night.

His conclusion as to what makes a business more successful than others was just as surprising as his method used to discover it:

"It's storytelling," he said, "whoever has the best story and tells it to the most people wins. It's more than just marketing or advertising. People want to be a part of something and if you can get the story right, they'll buy into it."

Since then Tom's continued on the same experimental path discovering what takes most people a lifetime to learn. He's worked for Blue Rubicon, the UK's #1 PR agency, simply to learn how it works; started a design business without a creative bone in his body just to learn about branding ("well, I may as well get paid to learn it", FullScream.com); and became a bespoke suit tailor - yes, you read that right - to learn how a traditional family-owned business can still thrive in today's world (MullenAndMullen.co.uk).

So when Tom said he had turned his attention to the mystery of money: how to get it, save it, and grow it; I knew he was serious and that whatever the result was, it would be great.

Money's Big Secret is better than I had ever expected. It's excellent.

Deepak Tailor,
Founder of LatestFreeStuff.co.uk
& Winner of BBC Dragon's Den

CHAPTER 1

> Hidden behind the disguise of mundane habits are cryptic clues that reveal much more. Watch carefully and note what you see, for what people do shows how they came to be.

Two years ago I was standing in my kitchen making a cup of tea. The water had boiled, the kettle had clicked and the teaspoon went clink, clink, clink. I sat down on the creaky wooden chair and held the slightly-too-hot-cup in my hand. Steam whispered to the air and as I slurped the first sip I smiled in memory of all the cups before. Except for one: my first.

Why, I wondered, do we continue to drink tea even though most of us do not enjoy our first cup? Similarly to coffee, wine and beer, we acquire a taste for these bitter and dry drinks, choosing them over what would probably have been more natural: fruit juice or milk.

Perhaps with tea it's the warm and awakening comfort it gives. After all, it has caffeine which wakes us up. However, other drinks do this too and they haven't found such a special place in our homes. Maybe tea is the tastiest hot drink of all but I'd disagree, hot chocolate is far tastier. What is it then? What is it that makes us drink up to eight cups per day?

I looked outside the misty French windows across to the back of my neighbour's house. I lived on a terraced row where houses stand back to back. When it's that wonderful time of day where dusk settles and lights turn on, you get a short glimpse into the world of others. Today they sat, the newly weds, also enjoying a cup of tea.

Somehow I felt part of their story. I was there when it was just the man, and there when the lady arrived. She moved in, they held a wedding reception and shortly afterwards a large, noticeable bump came to be. Throughout it all we had shared one daily ritual: the afternoon cup of tea.

There it was, the clue.

Tea is made in a social setting. Think of Grandma who you ask, "Can we talk?" and she replies, "I'll put the kettle on." When we make tea we often do it with and for others. We wait for the water to boil, the kettle to click, the teaspoon to clink. Then we chat.

We chat about everything and everyone. News, politics, neighbours, friends, lovers and money. We especially like to talk about money. How much things cost, what bargains we found, our plans to get rich.

Money, it turns out, is very similar to tea. It's not just a tool for spending as economists would like us to believe, but completely entwined with the social setting in which it's earned, saved, borrowed, lent and spent.

Do you remember ever winning or finding money? How did it make you feel? Most say it's exciting, that they feel lucky and triumphant.

With this 'easy' money, what did you spend it on? If it's a while ago you may not remember, but chances are you spent it on something fun rather than put it into your boring savings account.

Yet if you earned the same amount of money after a long week of hard graft would you be as likely to splurge? Probably not. How we earn money plays a large part in how we spend, save and invest it. That's why we have different pots and jars for savings.

I remember when I was young I cared for an old lady, Miss Bibby, for £2 an hour at the weekends. She would pay me in cash and I'd keep it in a tin slowly saving up for a computer (it took me four years). I also used to wash my neighbour's car for £5, but this went into a different jar for toy soldiers. Things haven't changed much since. Income from my job goes into a current account and income from other things such as book royalties and speaking events go into a separate account for holidays.

The fact that what money means to us depends upon the social setting in which it's earned and spent explains why 'dirty money' is said to burn a hole in your pocket: you spend it as quickly as possible. Furthermore, it's why we say some criminals 'launder' money.

People flitter between two opposite spectrums when it comes to money. They either ignore it completely and find the whole finance thing a bore - life is too short - or they obsess about interest rates and the state of the global economy.

Either way, it's discussed with friends over a cup of tea.

What doesn't happen though, is any sort of *action*. They love to debate tactics, strategies and their thinking behind decisions. Yet other than *not* doing anything, they rarely put those decisions to work. I'll show you in this book how not to be like them. Getting rich and learning about money isn't, as the media pundits promote, about eeny-weeny details, but about getting started now - as early as possible - and doing a few basic things regularly.

While we love to talk, it's at the cost of actually doing anything. People get a thrill out of nitpicking, saying "yes but", "what about", and "no", because for some mysterious reason it gives us satisfaction. I haven't figured out why yet but it's probably because of biology and psychology (sharing information is better for our collective survival), but money is not a natural thing. We invented it. In order to get it and be rich we must consciously take action and avoid the pleasure of arguing minor points. This is a small book that says what needs to be said and little more. I will reveal to you money's big secrets and armed with that knowledge help you pay off your debts, save more money and invest for a richer future.

Why is money so complicated?

Everyday we're bombarded with money-related advice. I'm constantly bamboozled at the quantity of stuff shared online, in print and on TV.

I say 'stuff' because most of it is waffle and little helps you become rich. 'Experts' describe the global economy: how Japan has negative interest rates, how the European Central Bank has launched quantitative what-not, how the Federal Reserve has upgraded the status of this and that and how the UK's deficit means we're all doomed or saved. I forget the details for, as you will discover, they're not important.

The fact is, financial experts mostly describe what they see. Graph goes up, graph goes down. Oil is high, oil is low. Then they try to interpret that graph and find some sort of future consequence. For example, the Government has printed more money so this should encourage banks to lend which is great for small businesses - or is it? Whatever the answer, none of it helps you save and invest money. Talking about how a British steel company will close leading to thousands of job cuts is much more enticing to readers than simple debt-cutting advice and how-to guides on setting up an automated savings plan: the long-term practical steps that will actually earn you money.

Those giving personal finance advice such as which Investment Saving Allowances (ISAs) you should save into and how to avoid this and that are always changing what they promote. It's as if you were trying to lose weight and your personal trainer puts you on a different programme every week. First, Atkins. Then the 5-2 fasting regime. Finally, no sugar, no carbs, no nothing. Then they wonder why we quit our new exercise regime within a month.

Philip Tetlock, author of *Expert Political Judgement: How Good Is It? How Can We Know?*, revealed how Financial 'experts' are to be avoided. He interviewed 284 people who made their living 'commenting or offering advice on political and economic trends.' He asked these experts to predict the likelihoods of certain events happening in the not too distant future. Things they supposedly had expertise in. He gathered 80,000 predictions and then waited to see what happened.

In the words of Nobel Prize winner Daniel Kahneman, 'the results were devastating'. The experts performed worse than if you or I had tossed a coin for every prediction. People who spend their entire lives reading, researching and earning a living from the study of a specific topic: economics and politics, did worse at guessing what was going to happen than if we had just placed an equal bet. Do you know what would happen if those experts followed their own financial advice? They'd go bankrupt.

And that's exactly what does happen to some. In 1996, John Graham and Campbell Harvey studied over two hundred financial advice newsletters over a 12.5 year period and found 94.5 percent of them had gone out of business. These money gurus and hot-stock pickers couldn't even keep their own doors open.

If you want to lose weight the solution is simple and all the little bits of contrary advice boil down to the same thing: exercise more, eat less. Guess what? It's the same with money.

Money's Big Secret

Most of us are not born rich. However, it's likely that as a reader of this book, you're in a place where you have access to good financial institutions, employment prospects, social security and at least the *opportunity* to get rich.

So why is it then that despite all of this, most of us don't get rich? What is money's big secret?

Forget the get-rich-quick stories. Very few achieve immediate wealth and when you hear of people that do it's usually because of survivorship bias: you only hear about the one successful businessperson, not the other 10,000 who failed. Instead of get-rich-quick stories remember this: money's first big secret is that it grows faster and faster with time.

Read the stories of Smart Sally and Dumb Dan:

Smart Sally lives in The Wirral, a wet and green peninsular of land in the North West of England, home once upon a time to James Bond actor

Daniel Craig and before that the Normans and the Romans.

When she was 25, Smart Sally started saving and investing £100 per month. She did this for 10 years, stopping when she was 35. She did nothing else and let her money grow. With an 8% rate of return, aged 65, her money grew to £200,061.

Now consider the story of Dumb Dan:

Dumb Dan lives in Chelsea. Supposedly it's the richest borough of the United Kingdom, home to the powerful and famous.

Dan started ten years after Sally, when he was 35 years old. He too invested £100 per month but did it for three times as long – 30 years - right up until he was 65. With the same 8% rate of return, his account became worth £149,036.

	Starting Age	Monthly Investment	Years	Total Return
Smart Sally	25	£100	10	£200,061
Dumb Dan	35	£100	30	£149,036

Smart Sally, despite only saving and investing for 10 years as opposed to Dumb Dan's 30 years, earned over £50,000 more than him. This is because she understood money's first big secret: it grows faster and faster with time. The single most important thing you can do to be rich is to start early.

Getting rich is something anyone can achieve. You simply need to start and invest for long-term.

> **Reading Numbers**
>
> When you read about Smart Sally and Dumb Dan, did you skim over the numbers? Most people do. Numbers are difficult to read in the context of a story. However, as this is a book about money, you have to get comfortable with them. Read the story again really try to focus on what the numbers mean.

List your ideas

To get started right now, list three ideas of how you can save a little bit of money from today. Three ideas. Doesn't have to be huge amounts, it can even be just £3 per day. Don't feel bad about writing on the book either, I don't mind. Go ahead and think of three ideas:

1. _____
2. _____
3. _____

List your excuses

Now list your excuses. Everyone has excuses. I want you to come up with twenty-five and list them here. Why can't you save an extra £3 per day?

1.
2.
3.
4.
5.
6.
7.
8.
9.
10.
11.
12.

13.
14.
15.
16.
17.
18.
19.
20.
21.
22.
23.
24.
25.

I often hear excuses such as: "It's the Government's fault that we're poor."

"We weren't given proper education."

"We're paying for the mistakes of the previous generation."

All of this is true. Yes, the Government does not do enough to encourage saving. Yes, we were not taught financial responsibility at school. And yes, the previous generation enjoyed the longest period of wealth creation in the history of mankind and left us with a treeless world.

However, not one of the excuses on your list will help you get rich. Why? Because no one is listening. And no one will ever listen. While you moan and pass blame onto the Government, others are out there saving their £3 a day and following the example of Smart Sally. That's how much she saved: £3 a day (well, £3.33 technically). I'm not going to swaddle you like a baby and tell you everything's going to be OK, because if you don't take action, it won't be. There is only one person who can help you and that's yourself. You have to ignore your list of excuses and focus on your first list: how to start saving money today. Money's first big secret (it has two) is to start early.

You may think that you need to get other financial matters sorted first. This is very common and often because of the plethora of mixed financial advice we receive. We're told to re-negotiate our mortgage rates (if you're 'lucky' enough to have a mortgage), shift our credit card debts around, open cashback bank accounts, use high interest savings accounts, put money into mutual funds and to choose 'hot stocks'. We become paralysed and put off our decision to save and invest money until later: the next payday or, when you have a cushion of cash or when you get a promotion.

It doesn't have to be £1,000 a month. It can be £3 a day. What's important is that you focus on what you can change yourself and get started today.

Soon you'll be able to automate your finances but the first step is a change in your behaviour. Every month you'll automatically save and invest what you can afford which means your money will grow over the long-term without you having to worry about it. You can go back to work and focus on getting a pay rise or starting a business.

From now on, there are no more excuses. You are committed to saving and investing your money and you recognise money's first big secret is that it grows faster and faster with time so you have to start now, right now.

Why do you want to be rich?

Why do you want to be rich? To live a better life, right?

It may sound straightforward but what does that exactly mean to you? Is it to have two children, own a house in the countryside and to drive an electric car? Is it to go on holiday every month of the year? Or is it to have a fully stocked wine cellar?

Usually people want to be rich for one or two exact reasons but rarely want *everything* in the world. I, for example, am a bookworm and love the crisp fold of a new, more expensive, hardback than reading off a Kindle. My dream is to recline in a reading chair and to enjoy a private library full of hardbacks. I know I could get them cheaper but that's not the point. The Ferrari outside? Not interested. Traveling constantly around the world? Not for me.

Your idea of a rich life may be the opposite. You may not care for books but get giddy with excitement for globetrotting and exploring the deepest canyons and highest mountains. You may dream of drifting a Ferrari around Silverstone or sailing a yacht in the Mediterranean.

Think about what you *really* want.

If you want to clamber through Brazilian rainforests and discover new species of animals, write it down. If you want to open a coffee shop, note that down too. Unfortunately these are long-term saving goals and you can only do them once you have money.

Most human misery is caused by inward thinking: looking at what we don't have and how far away we are from where we'd like to be. While it's important to have long-term goals such as those above, they're usually too far away to keep our determination and will power going. Instead, it's better to use what we enjoy right now, here in the present, as a tool for keeping our savings and investments on track.

Ask yourself, what are two or three things you really enjoy every day? Is it the freshly brewed caffe latte on the way to work? Is it cooking your children a tasty dinner they lick from their plates? Or is it quad-ply aloe vera loo roll?

If these are the things you enjoy on a daily basis then make a conscious decision to enjoy them.

What do I mean? When talking about how to save money, most frugal experts will tell you to strip back on everything: take a flask to work. Cook frozen meat and vegetables. Use basics loo roll.

They don't understand human psychology. If saving and investing makes your life miserable, you're not going to do it. When has punishment ever beaten encouragement as a method of learning?

It's better to consciously decide what you enjoy on a day-to-day basis and to allow yourself those things as rewards. Cut back ruthlessly on everything else. Life is too short to skimp on *everything* for a future you may not have. If there's something that gives you great amounts of daily satisfaction, keep it. Use it as a way of giving yourself a pat on the back for saving on other things. Spend to your advantage.

Learn how to do this and you'll be drinking your caffe latte and *smiling* at the money you just handed over. You will know that this caffe latte is what you enjoy the most each and every day. You will take that first glorious sip and the smell of freshly ground coffee beans will make you think of chocolate and golden rays of sunshine rising over the Tuscan hills of Italy on a cool and blue-skied morning. You will enjoy your coffee in the full knowledge that you have cut back on everything else, that you have saved and invested towards your long-term goal, but that here, right now, you're going to enjoy what life has to offer.

List one thing you get the most enjoyment from on a daily basis:

1.

This is called your Single Spending Allowance (SSA). Prioritise your spending on this and cut back like a Samurai warrior on everything else. Consciously enjoy the things you love and stop spending on what's not important.

This is not a sexy book

If most experts followed their own financial advice they'd be at a loss. There are very few media titles that have, over the long-term, beaten the market average. The Investor's Chronicle is one that has, however, and that's because it understands money's first big secret: it's a long-term game and you have to start early. The magazine is over 150 years old and the editorial team take a long-term view which is a rarity in the cluttered media world.

Most other financial media outlets and experts share what they think is sexy, not sensible. 'Hot stocks', high performance funds, bio-tech. These things are rife with risk and a recipe for ruin. You'd be wise to avoid them.

Why do experts give sexy rather than sensible tips? It's because they're in the media and they sell magazines or page views. They're not betting on the stock markets based on their own advice - if they did, they'd be bankrupt - they're trying to sell you a copy of their publication. Furthermore, as Philip Tetlock revealed in his study of predictions, experts can be over-confident in themselves.

This is not a sexy book. You're not going to learn about complicated investment strategies.
Even 'mutual funds' are too sexy for me. Instead, I'll show you how to automatically invest and diversify your savings. You'll discover it's no more complicated than subscribing to a gym membership but that anyone can get the same returns as professional investors.

Sexy choices don't make you rich. Sensible long-term decisions do.

CHAPTER 2

The Truth About Money: What Is It?

I've already revealed to you money's first big secret: if you invest wisely it can grow faster and faster with time and so you have to start early and play the long-term game. Money also has a second big secret and it's a little bit more intriguing.

As we've already discovered with drinking tea, things are rarely as simple as they seem. We don't just drink tea because we like the taste (most of us prefer hot chocolate, after all), we drink it because of social reasons.

The same can be said of many things. It's why products in a car boot sale are not as attractive as those displayed neatly in a shop. It's why Ikea catalogues use photographs of a lifestyle, not just a list of products. And it's why we have different piggy banks, jars and pots of money for different things.

We're not economic calculators who list the costs and benefits of every purchase. We are emotional beings who get upset, angry and excited.

Men in suits like to teach that money is a tool for trade; it's easier to use money to get what we want than to barter.

Adam Smith, the man who invented the theory of economics, suggested that before money people used to trade a haircut for a pig, a pig for two loaves of bread and two loaves of bread for a wife. Or something like that. Regardless of specifics, he argued money was created to help with exchange. His thinking has gone on to define 20th and 21st century economics.

There is just a little problem with this theory of the invention of money. He argued this without one shred of evidence. He said people bartered for everything. When you think about it, it's pretty bonkers. If you lived in a small community of no more than 150 people, all of whom you knew intimately, would you demand that in exchange for a haircut you should get a pig, even if you had no use for a pig?

It's unlikely. Imagine inviting a friend over for dinner and asking them to pay for it. You just wouldn't.

Anthropologists such as David Graeber of the London School of Economics have since argued that there is no documented evidence that people ever lived with the bartered system Smith suggests. Right up until now, even in small tribal societies that do not have money, this system of bartered exchange has not been found to exist.

In small communities such as these, if you wanted a haircut, I'd give you a haircut. I would not demand a pig in exchange. We would have known each other for years and as such, would be friends if not family. If I ever found myself in need of a pig and you had a surplus of them, I would feel happy to come by and ask you for one. For the same reasons you'd probably not think twice in giving me one.

When society is small we remember our debts. Examples of this can be found in many instances today: friends host dinners, parents walk each other's children to school, rounds of drinks are bought in pubs. Can you think of an example where you share something with friends?

When you share things with friends and family you consider them to be gestures of good will. You don't ask for money. Yet, you would expect your friends to be willing to return the gesture in kind at some point in the future. This is where we get to the second of money's big secrets: money was created not a tool of exchange but as a measurement of debt.

When society grows and the quantity of trade increases it becomes difficult to keep track of all these gestures of goodwill. If your friend came back for dinner the following day, and the following day after that again, without giving anything in return, you may start to feel frustrated. Similarly, if ten friends then came over every day, you'd feel taken advantage of. Go a bit further and imagine twenty people come every day: you're essentially a restaurant. As small societies began to experience this they created tools to keep track of debt. For example, scratching a tally on a clay tablet every time someone comes over for food.

This, as Graeber explains, was the advent of money and it's for this use we have evidence for. Not as a tool of exchange but as a measure of debt.

Our whole world economy is built upon this. When we hand someone money we are giving a token of debt. All forms of money - coins, notes, bearer bonds and digital currencies - are essentially the same thing: a promise to give something in return. Understanding this fact has profound implications in how you think about money.

When you hold money, you are holding a piece of debt. On all British notes there is a little message printed. It reads, the 'Bank of England... I promise to pay the bearer on demand the sum of five / ten / twenty / fifty pounds'. The Bank of England is saying that this note you're holding is not actually money, but a promise of the debt it owes you.

Cash is simply a token with which you can use to retrieve that debt from the Bank of England. Up until 1931, you could walk to the Bank of England on Threadneedle Street in Central London and legally demand a portion of gold of the equivalent value. However, due to the heavy and impractical nature of gold, few ever did and instead contracts were written, for example, 'so and so owns X amount of gold'.

In the run up to 1931 other countries which held British currency lost confidence in the economy and started asking for their gold. So much gold, in fact, the country almost ran out which would have meant Government bankruptcy. To avoid disaster, the ruling party decided to change the law and said money was no longer tied to gold. One can no longer convert it into the precious metal. Since then, money is only what you believe it to be, a promise from one person to another.

The statement on our cash, 'I promise to pay the bearer on demand...' is more of a historical feature, a relic of the past. That money cannot be exchanged for something solid like gold has deep implications, but what's important for us is to recognise our cash as unclaimed promises. Those notes in your purse, those coins in your jar: they are all IOUs and until you invest them, you're not getting anything in return.

You may think that having wads of cash is a good thing. After all, it means you can buy stuff, invest, or donate. However, for as long as you are holding on to cash - those unclaimed promises - you are not getting anything in return. In fact, as you hold on to it more and more cash is being printed and the value of your money decreases. This is inflation.

Money's second big secret is that it's a token of debt: what's owed to you. Unless you buy something or invest your savings, you won't get anything in return. If you do, you can enjoy a beautiful thing called 'compound interest' which is the technical name of money's first big secret: that it can grow faster and faster with time.

In order to collect your promises and put your money to work, you must first make sure you do not own any expensive debt. This is because the cost of debt, especially on credit cards, is nearly always more than what you can earn with investment.

CHAPTER 3

Credit cards pay for most of life's biggest purchases such as cars, weddings and holidays. However they can also turn us into debt slaves struggling to pay off the ever growing mountain of interest.

Isn't it strange that it's the indebted who feel guilty? Credit card companies lend a paltry amount of money, charge extortionate interest rates and fees, and then when a debtor struggles to pay it's them that feels bad!

Something's wrong here. Our moral compass must be off. Brushing bills under the rug, hiding from bailiffs and struggling to feed a family because of extreme interest rates is not right. You can beat the credit cards and now's the time you will.

Before you save and invest your money - those unclaimed promises - you need to be rid of your debt. Credit cards are often the most expensive kind of debt which is why you should start with them. If you don't have credit card debt it's worth you reading this chapter anyway for the same principles apply to loans and mortgages.

The average interest rate for a credit card is 18.9% a year. If you have a £1,000 of credit card debt, this means you will be charged £189 of interest in year one making your new debt £1,189.

Credit card companies make profit from these interest charges. The longer it takes you to pay off the debt, the more interest you pay and the more profit goes into their pockets instead of yours.

If you left your £1,000 credit card debt untouched for 5 years, it would grow to £2,553.98, more than double the original amount.

Debt	Interest	Years	New Debt
£1,000	18.9%	5	£2,553.98

Credit card companies want you to be in debt. That's their business model. They want you to be trying to pay it off but never quite succeeding. They win when you lose: making you a debt slave is in their interests - and it's completely legal.

You want to tackle credit card debt as fast as possible and to do that you just have to get started.

Discover your debt

Jacqui
Jacqui laughed as she waved her hand in the air throwing the question of how much debt she had away into the corner.

"I really don't know," she said.
"Well let's start with what's in your purse." I replied.

Jacqui rummaged for her brown leather purse and popped it open. Her cards were neatly arranged, one in each slot. I took them out and laid them on the table. She had two credit cards.

"Tell me about these," I said.

Two years ago Jacqui and her husband had bought a new house in York. It was their first house and it took all their savings and more to put down the deposit. They'd bought a house that was in need of some "love and care", but soon found out it needed more than just a lick of paint. As they had no more savings and had got the maximum mortgage they could afford, Jacqui made the decision to take out a credit card. It was interest-free for a year which made it an attractive offer and they were sure with a bit of thriftiness and hopefully a joint pay rise they could pay it off. Just under a year later they had taken out a second credit card.

    Jacqui was expecting her first child and having used their credit limit on the first card to do repairs on the house, now needed money in preparation of their newborn. On top of that, unfortunately Jacqui's husband had lost his job, which meant they were struggling to keep up with mortgage repayments too. Selling the house would have taken too long so understandably they took out the second card.

"I wish we had never bought the house," Jacqui

said, but then she looks over at her daughter and smiles as she gnaws into a fluffy ball. There's never any regret when it comes to providing for the love of children.

We spent the next hour calling the credit cards using the telephone number on the back and re-discovering the debt Jacqui now had. It had grown to about £15,000 and she was being asked to pay £230 per month simply in interest repayments.

Simon

I once met an IT professional with a secret: he was £2,500 overdrawn. We were at a Samba party and somehow found ourselves ranting about the cost of living in London. He described his feeling of being trapped in a cycle of debt and after quite a bit of probing revealed his secret of debt. I offered to help and we met a week later in a Costa coffee shop on Southampton Row.

Simon explained that every month he would get paid and his overdraft would be reduced but that it was never enough to clear it. After rent and living expenses he'd be back at the same level of debt.

"How long has it been like this?" I asked.
"About three years," he replied.

As we spoke I was confused why he wasn't more frustrated about the debt he had. He complained about the cost of rent, travel and utilities but never about the actual debt he had.

"How much does the overdraft cost you?"
"What do you mean?" he asked.

Simon had not realised that an overdraft was the same as a loan or credit card in the sense that you have to pay interest. He sat up when I told him this and almost spilt his coffee.

"I thought my overdraft was free? I thought I had a free limit and then I get fined?"

We called his bank (using the number on the back of the card) and discovered his debt: the overdraft cost him 19.9% interest and he had been fined £75 every month for going into it. Not once had he ever received a letter or phone call from his bank explaining the situation. They were simply taking money from his account and unless he rummaged through his transaction history he would never have seen it. Simon started to argue with the representative on the phone and I took it out of his hand and hung up. That wasn't going to solve anything.

Rowena
Rowena could not even remember what credit cards or debt she had. Years ago, she said, she had cut them up and thrown them at a bailiff when he came knocking on her door. I imagine he had stood there startled as bits of sharp plastic hit

him in the face. Knowing Rowena, she would have screamed him out of the entire neighbourhood too. She was strong like that and always made me laugh.

It had been a long time since she had last opened a bill and indeed they seemed to have stopped coming (if credit card companies can't get their money back they sell your debt to other companies for cheap, who then use forceful tactics like bailiffs to intimidate you into paying. Yet if they fail, eventually, it's possible they all give up – usually after seven years). However Rowena had since got a new job, several pay rises and was in a position to start saving and investing money. She said she wanted to open a nail salon but was worried her bad credit history would make it difficult for her to take out a loan if needed.

To discover her debt we used two credit check tools: Experian.co.uk and Equifax.co.uk. They cost about £2 each. Put in all the addresses you have lived in and they match those addresses to outstanding debts.

Rowena's debts were not as bad as she had thought considering so much time had passed and they usually grow every year. They stood at £12,000.

Credit card debt is often the most expensive but as these stories attest, it's important to discover *all* of your debt. Remember overdrafts charge interest too, as well as hefty fines.

Usually the money you pay to service your debts is more than anything you can get from saving and investing, so focus on paying off your debt first. To do that you must find out how much debt you own, what interest it's charging, and whether you're being fined for late or missed repayments. The easiest way to achieve this is to call the number on the back of your cards and ask.

Create a table similar to the one below to discover your debt. Write down every credit card, loan, overdraft and other debt you have: the name, the total amount, the interest they each charge and then what that costs you. For example, if I have credit card debt of £1,000 and it's charging me 18.9% interest that costs me £189 per year. This figure represents the interest payments only, not any money actually going towards paying off the debt. Turn the page to see a table for you to fill in.

	Name	Amount	Interest %	Yearly £
E.g.	Credit Co.	£1,000	18.9%	£189
1.				
2.				
3.				
4.				
Total				

Armed with this information you now have a clear financial snapshot of your debt situation. It may be a shock to you how much you're throwing away every year in interest payments and undoubtedly you'll be pretty mad.

This table often provokes an intense reaction when I create it in person with people in money trouble. It might be the first time they've seen all their debts laid out together and some cry at the situation they find themselves it. Seeing it together in this way is the first big step to being debt-free and then saving and investing your money towards a happy future. It's a huge psychological step to line debt up like this because it's accepting the problem, admitting it to yourself, and acknowledging that you have to beat it.

At this point I normally put the kettle on for a second brew.

Pay the most expensive debt first

Not too long ago I was in Barcelona for a crash course in cooking tapas. My teacher Matías, upon learning what I was working on, asked for some advice. Unlike the English, he was more than happy to speak about his money trouble loudly in front of everyone.

"I have thousands of debt," he declared, "credit cards, loans, banks... with everything I have debt. But with so many debts, how do I pay it off? Which do I choose?"

Different debts charge you different amounts of interest. As you want to get rid of them as fast as possible you should pay off the most expensive debt first: that which charges the most interest.
    However, you must remember to keep paying the minimum on all your debts. You do not want to miss minimum repayments and be hit with heavy fees. Pay the minimum repayments on all of your debts and put any additional money you have towards paying off the most expensive debt first.
    This explanation provoked a response from a fellow tapas-student who shared the view voiced quite often online. His argument described something called the Snowball Method.
    The Snowball Method is where you pay the minimums on all the cards, but pay more money to the card with the *lowest* balance first - the one

that will allow you to pay it off first. It may not be the most *expensive*, but is the *smallest* debt you hold.

By paying off the smallest debts first you can cross them off your list faster giving you a little emotional uplift and encouragement to tackle the next biggest debt. While in total you will end up spending more time and money paying off all your debts, you may be more likely to achieve it.

Either way don't spend more than 5 minutes thinking about it. Choose a method - pay off the most expensive debts first, or the smallest - and stick with it. As I said to Matías who is now debt-free, what matters is that you start paying down that debt today.

Visit tomchurch.co.uk/r/debt-calculator/ to work out exactly how long it will take you to pay off your debts.

You're a customer: Get cheaper interest rates

On the back of your credit card is a telephone number. It's probably the most powerful telephone number you have right now and all you have to do is call it.

Call your credit card company and ask for a cheaper interest rate. Half of the time they'll say yes. Half! It's as if you were tossing a coin. For a five-minute telephone call that may save you hundreds of pounds, it's worth it. Here are some positive experiences money savers have had:

- **Barclaycard** - reduced from 29.9% to 9.9%
- **HSBC** - reduced from 16.9% to 4.9% for six months
- **Lloyds** - reduced from 18.9% to 6.9%

Remember, while you may be indebted to a bank or credit card company, you are still their *customer*. You are paying them money for a financial *product*. In the same was as you can negotiate mobile phone contracts, television subscriptions, utility bills... You can do the same with interest rates.

How to negotiate cheaper interest rates
The best telephone script I have found to help you get lower interest rates is than from Ramit Sethi of *I Will Teach You To Be Rich*:

YOU: Hi, I'm going to be paying off my credit card debt more aggressively beginning next week and I'd like a lower interest rate.

Credit Card Rep: Uh, why?

YOU: I've decided to be more aggressive about paying off my debt, and that's why I'd like a lower interest rate. Other cards are offering me rates below half what you're offering. Can you lower my rate?

Credit Card Rep: Hmm... After reviewing your account, I'm afraid we can't offer you a lower interest rate. We can offer you a credit limit increase, however.

YOU: No, that won't work for me. Like I mentioned, other credit cards are offering me zero percent introductory rates for twelve months, as well as interest rates below half what you're offering. I've been a customer for X years, and I'd prefer not to switch my balance over to a low-interest card. Can you match the other credit card rates, or can you go lower?

Credit Card Rep: I see... Hmm, let me pull something up here. Fortunately, the system is suddenly letting me offer you a reduced interest rate. That is effective immediately.

This works over half the time and is defi[n]
worth a shot. Martin Lewis, founder of
MoneySavingExpert.com, said, 'It's truly
asking can work... Be confident, be polite, be
charming and try to think of a reason your rate
should be cheaper. It's amazing what deals
customer-service reps have the power to
authorise.'

If you have debt of £10,000 and paying 16.9%
interest per year, that's £1,690. If you can reduce
the interest rate to just 9.9%, it becomes £990. A
huge saving of £700. The more you can cut your
interest rates the better. Go through your table of
debts and call every one to try and reduce your
interest rates. You have nothing to lose, only
thousands to gain.

Debt	Interest Rate	Interest
£10,000	16.9%	£1,690
£10,000	9.9%	£990

What about balance transfers?

You may have read about balance transfers:
moving your credit card debts around to get
cheaper interest rates. This is also called card-
shuffling and I'm not a fan.
    It works by taking out a new credit card,
usually one with an interest-free introductory
offer and moving your debts into it. This way you

compile your debts into one and make them as cheap as possible.

However, this card-shuffling technique is fraught with sneaky tactics from credit card companies and in my experience working with people to reduce their debts, often they are tricked into paying more, or end up spending too much time researching the best deals rather than actually paying off any debt.

Credit cards can charge you balance transfer fees, usually about 3%, so that it costs you to move your debt around. Secondly, you must remember to pay it off or move it again before the higher interest rate kicks in at the end of the introductory offer and you usually still have to pay the interest rate on purchases with the card.

Paying off debts is like a huge psychological war. Things like balance transfers are just more battles you're giving yourself to fight. It's hard enough to admit the problem and to confront it. In my experience working with people, keeping it simple works best. This means changing your spending habits and earning more to pay it back. Calling up the credit card companies and negotiating cheaper interest rates is the best way to reduce the cost of your debt today.

CHAPTER 4

Why do we feel poor?

I felt poor for a long time. I wasn't really, but the feeling was real. It started when I moved to London for University. I couldn't afford my student rent so I had to get a job as a barman at night. I worked to three in the morning, cycled home, had a few hours sleep then went to lectures. I did this five nights a week.

My academic results weren't good in the first year. I knew the night job was unsustainable so I switched job. I got a job as a manager at a health practice during the day, skipped lectures and studied at night. It felt awful. I was working all day to pay for accommodation so that I could go to University, which I couldn't go to because I was working all day.

It was a trap and I had to get out. I studied hard in the evenings and completed my degree in two years instead of three. I got a good grade and ticked the whole 'University thing' off my life.

My peers were in awe and I'd love to say I felt proud, but in truth I felt ashamed. I didn't go to my graduation ceremony because I felt I hadn't earned it. Perhaps I could not face looking at my professor in the eye for the first time, or perhaps University was the trap I had just escaped from and I didn't want to go back.

Either way, I felt poor. However, if you had met me on the street you wouldn't think I was poor.

You'd see a young man in new clothes, probably listening to music on his iPhone. You'd see him living in Central London, enjoying the company of friends and cycling off to work. That certainly doesn't convey the image of being poor.

Very few in Britain are as impoverished in the same sense as those poor nations where millions cling to hunger as a defence against starvation. We don't have to think about whether we've chlorinated the water, taken our antimalarials or sanitised our waste. Nor do we have to worry whether we have any water, pharmaceuticals or food. It's all there if we want it, running through taps, dispensed at NHS hospitals, handed out at food banks. We're not going to die.

    Yet, we can certainly *feel* poor. Trapped, even. The normal path of living a rich life doesn't make sense to us either. Ellen Goodman, an American journalist, once amusingly observed:

'Normal is getting dressed in clothes that you buy for work and driving through traffic in a car that you are still paying for - in order to get the job you need to pay for the clothes and the car, and the house you leave vacant all day so you can afford to live in it.'

    We can *feel* poor but not look it.
    Cheap clothes, electronics and beauty mask the underlying truth. If a tourist of an impoverished nation were to walk along the bustling High

Street of Lewisham, one of London's poorest boroughs, she would see fashion shops, coffee chains and mobile phone stores. She would say, 'these people' are truly fortunate.

As Michael Harrington wrote in *The Other America*, 'it is easier to be decently dressed than it is to be decently housed, fed, or doctored. Even people with terribly depressed incomes can look prosperous.'

While today's poor in developed countries may not be clinging to hunger, 'That does not change the fact that tens of millions… are, at this very moment, maimed in body and spirit, existing at levels beneath those necessary for human decency. If these people are not starving, they are hungry and sometimes fat with hunger, for that is what cheap foods do. They are without adequate housing and education and medical care.'

You might be wearing shoes, perhaps even a stylishly cut suit or dress, and yet have the pain of being poor. Harrington writes, 'It almost seems as if the affluent society had given out costumes to the poor so that they would not offend the rest of society with the sight of rags'.

Looking rich but being poor is nothing new and it's important for the wealthy to understand this. George Orwell, the author of literary classics such as *Animal Farm* and *1984* once wrote in a lesser known book, *The Road To Wigan Pier*, a description of northern English mining towns in the early 1930s. Poverty was extreme with lavatories a hundred yards from your home and shared by up to 36 people. No hot water and no baths. Unbearable working conditions and horrendously low pay. And yet, Orwell writes of how 'luxury' items such as new clothes were enjoyed. It's worth reading the description in full:

'[The poor] don't necessarily lower their standards by cutting out luxuries and concentrating on necessities; more often it is the other way about - the more natural way, if you come to think of it. Hence the fact that in a decade of unparalleled depression, the consumption of all cheap luxuries has increased. The two things that have probably made the greatest difference of all are the movies and the mass-production of cheap smart clothes since the war. The youth who leaves school at fourteen and gets a blind-alley job is out of work at twenty, probably for life; but for two pounds ten on the hire-purchase system he can buy himself a suit which, for a little while and at a little distance, looks as though it had been tailored in Savile Row. The girl can look like a fashion plate at an even lower price. You may have three halfpence in your pocket and not a prospect in the world, and only the corner of a leaky bedroom to go home to; but in your new clothes you can stand on the street corner, indulging in a private daydream of yourself.'

Today, we may have central heating, water

flowing freely from our taps, an NHS to look after us when we're unwell, job seeker's allowance when we're unemployed and access to a feast of foods and clothes for little money, but that doesn't mean we can't feel poor.

Primarily this is because of debt and rent traps. To be paid every month and have nothing left to save or invest. To have no future to look forward to. To have no hope. Rents go up, debts increase, pay stagnates. With every passing moment we're squeezed a little bit more, milked a little harder.

Modern poverty is disguised in debt. Unlike the coal miners of the 1930s, we have access to easy credit. Thousands of pounds if we like, with zero per cent interest for the first year or more. And when you're at rock bottom, struggling to pay your rent, perhaps with a baby to feed, this 'free' credit can be a life send.

If invested wisely it can help you get out of poverty. For example, a reader of mine whom I shall call Freddie, lived in the rolling green hills of Wiltshire and didn't have access to many jobs. While he wanted to move into a bigger town, he couldn't because he had to look after his mum at home. The bills were piling up and he was quickly slipping into the red. I suggested he take out a loan and buy a second hand car. This enabled him to access a larger job market which, after a short while allowed him to pay off the loan and then sustainably stay at home with mum.

This is a great use of credit. Very often however, it doesn't end up how we want it to.

Richard, from Bristol, started with good intentions. He needed a 'bridging' loan to cover his rent while he waited for his pay. Because of an attractive introductory offer (interest-free for twelve months) he took out more than he needed. Richard paid his rent with the loan, got paid from work a fortnight later and paid back the loan. However he had also spent credit on other things too. Impulse purchases.

Two months later he found himself in a familiar situation. He didn't have enough money to pay his rent because he had to pay back the impulse purchases. He had to take out more credit and the debt increased. Then the high interest rate kicked in and he found himself in real trouble - that's when we met.

Poverty in developed countries such as ours is different. It's not clinging on to starvation nor working in abysmal conditions. Wealthy people think the poor just complain and don't realise how good they have it. In fact, they can't see modern poverty for it's invisible and often attached to the future: poverty is our debt and debt is paid back over time. It forces us into a life we do not want and removes our freedom.

When you're young and able to work this isn't so much a problem. You work, get paid, pay off a little chunk of your debt. You work some more, get paid, pay off another little chunk of your debt. You keep doing this for as long as you are able to get work. Yet because you're paying back this debt, you're unable to save and unable to invest. Your poverty is pushed forward into the future when the day comes that you cannot work. Nobody notices or says anything because it's invisible. As far as anyone else is concerned, you're wearing nice new clothes and have an iPhone. Things must be good, right? Wrong.

Money's second big secret is that it's a token of debt. You are either a creditor or a debtor. If you're a debtor then you don't have freedom. You're working for someone else's future.

My goal with this book is twofold: first, to show you the ugly truth of debt. How fast it grows and how it can take away your freedom. Second, as my American friends would say, how to stick it to the man. I don't want to live in a world where everyone's life experiences are dictated by creditors. I don't want you to trudge off to work only to pay all your earnings to someone else. It makes you depressed which, in turn, makes me depressed. To be robbed like this with extortionate interest rates seems to me a return to medieval times. I want us to be free. I want to give you your future back. If you get rid of your debt, save and invest, you can have that.

In the next part of this book you'll learn:

1. How to save money: The 3-30 Money Diet
2. How to create an automated money system
3. How investment 'experts' are consistently wrong
4. How to stay rich over 2,000 years
5. How to diversify your investments and focus on the long-term

*****

Please review this book on Amazon

If you've turned this many pages already I hope that means you're enjoying *Money's Big Secret*. Which topic have you found most interesting?

Please take a moment and write a review on Amazon. Reviews help to spread the word. I would love for this to become a personal finance classic, a book that helps people understand the truth about money, clear their debts and to save and invest for a happy future.

Either way, thank you for your time and for reading *Money's Big Secret*,

Tom

*****

PART II

CHAPTER 5

How to change your mindset

The first step to escaping rent traps, debt, and poverty is to change your mindset about what it means to be poor.

In the previous chapter I kept repeating that we *feel* poor. That poverty is a *feeling*. I want you to get rid of that. Being in debt is confusing, yes. David Graeber, Anthropologist at the London School of Economics and author of *Debt: The First 5,000 Years*, explains,

> 'If one looks at the history of debt… one finds that the majority of human beings hold simultaneously that (1) paying back money one has borrowed is a simple matter of morality, and (2) anyone in the habit of lending money is evil.'

We feel obliged to pay back debt and at the same time we despise the people who lent it to us. This makes us angry and disgruntled. We lose our freedom and *feel* poor.

Poverty in developed countries is largely a mindset and I want you to get rid of it. Instead, think of it just as debt. Black and white. You owe

X amount of money and you're going to pay it back. Or, if you're not in debt but just struggling, you need X amount of money to be able to breathe.

Remember: You are alive! You have access to water and if you need it, food and medication. If you're really in trouble you can go to a food bank. You can get Job Seeker's Allowance which is enough to keep the blood pumping (but little more) and the internet means we can re-train ourselves to learn any new skills.

To see what I mean about changing your mindset let's look at the world's truly poor, those on $1 per day. Abhijit Banerjee and Esther Duflo are two world renowned economists who have dedicated their lives to studying such impoverished people. Their pioneering book, *Poor Economics*, uncovered surprising revelations about the poor and life on less than $1 a day.

Time and time again, foreign aid and loans on offer to the poor were *rejected*. People on $1 per day often rejected money. It didn't seem to make sense. If the poor simply took the money and invested it into a bit of education, health and housing, they could get better jobs and escape poverty.

One story shows why everything depends upon your mindset:

Abhijit and Esther, the economists, went to a village called Hafret Ben Tayeb in Morocco to try and find out why the poor were not accepting financial help. They were received by Allal Ben Sedan, the father of three sons and two daughters, all adults.

> 'He had four cows, one donkey, and eighty olive trees. One of his sons worked in the army; another tended to the animals; the third was mostly idle (his main activity was harvesting snails when they were in season). We asked Ben Sedan whether he would want to take a loan to buy some more cows, which his idle son could take care of. He explained that his field was too small - if he bought more cows they would have nowhere to graze. Before leaving, we asked him if there was anything else he could do with a loan. He replied, "No, nothing. We have enough. We have cows, we sell them, we sell the olives. That is enough for our family."'

For Ben Sedan, money was not what made his life rich. He loved his farm and his olive trees, and they were enough to make him happy.

The following story told by David Graeber illustrates the point of mindset perfectly. It's a conversation between a missionary and a Samoan, whom he discovered lying on the beach:

"Look at you! You're just wasting your life away, lying around like that." Said the missionary.
"Why? What do you think I should be doing?" replied the Samoan.
"Well, there are plenty of coconuts all around here. Why not dry some copra and sell it?"
"And why would I want to do that?"
"You could make a lot of money. And with the money you make, you could get a drying machine, and dry copra faster, and make even more money."
"Okay. And why would I want to do that?"
"Well, you'd be rich. You could buy land, plant more trees, expand operations. At that point, you wouldn't even have to do the physical work anymore, you could just hire a bunch of other people to do it for you."
"Okay. And why would I want to do that?"
"Well, eventually, with all that copra, land, machines, employees, with all that money - you could retire a very rich man. And then you

wouldn't have to do anything. You could just lie on the beach all day."

The irony of the story is that the Samoan was already lying on the beach all day.

You need to change your mindset. Perhaps you only have a part-time job and feel you'd be richer with a full-time job. Know that some people would kill for the free time you have. Perhaps you only have a bicycle and feel you'd be richer with a car. Know that car owners are usually paying off loans and have insurance, petrol and annual MOTs to pay. Perhaps you're overweight and feel you can only afford bad foods. Know that eggs and bananas are the most cost-effective nutrition you can get.
    Whatever is holding you back, whatever ill-thoughts or resentments, you have to leave them there and move forward. Everything is a mindset. From this point on you are no longer poor. You are working towards a future and you're going to see your numbers improve. You're going to adopt a new mindset, one that sees your lack of things as an advantage: possessions tie you down. You're going to see your free time as an opportunity to learn and re-train. You're going to become like Ben Sedan who looked at his olive trees and

said, "Hey, you know what? They're enough for me."

Like the wise Samoan who enjoyed the beach, you're going to decide what gives you pleasure and you're going to enjoy it. Spend whatever you want on it. But everything else? That can go.

Cut back and wake up. Become aware of how you spend your money, how much you're giving away to profiteering companies, and subsequently and how much you can save. To achieve this, let me show you The 3-30 Money Diet.

CHAPTER 6

It was my third day without food. I was reading a book called *The Man Who Planted Trees* by Jean Giono, the story of a quiet French shepherd who every day planted a hundred acorn seeds. His name was Elzéard Bouffier and 'for three years he had been planting trees in this wilderness. He had planted one hundred thousand. Of the hundred thousand, twenty thousand had sprouted. Of the twenty thousand he still expected to lose about half, to rodents or to the unpredictable designs of Providence. There remained ten thousand oak trees to grow where nothing had grown before.' The story was one of the most beautiful I had ever read and for the first time in a long while, I cried.

It was in that moment I decided to write *Money's Big Secret.* I saw the similarity between it and how you have a take a long-term approach with money too. That if you save and plant those acorns, you too can have a forest with which you can live a free and happy life.

At the time I was experimenting with fasting. I had gone three days without food, drinking only water and was feeling a little bit woozy. Inspired by a letter written by Roman Stoic philosopher and statesman, Seneca, I was practicing poverty.

Seneca believed most of our life is driven by fear: fear of failure, fear of poverty, fear of death. How often have you put off a decision, what you really want to do, because of the worry you wouldn't be able to afford it or that you'd lose everything?

Seneca explained that to face our fears, we should practice them. In regards to failure and poverty he wrote, 'set aside a certain number of days, during which you shall be content with the scantiest and cheapest fare, with course and rough dress, saying to yourself the while: "Is this the condition that I feared?"'

Having read that letter I wondered, *if I lost everything, what's the worst that could happen*? I gathered it would be not being able to afford any food, and so following his advice I decided to fast. For the first time in my life I would go for a week without anything to eat.

The first day was the hardest. I was very conscious that I was doing this new thing and kept asking myself, *am I hungry yet? What about now? And now?*

Constant questioning of whether or not I was hungry made me oversensitive to my stomach and any little rumble was taken to mean a great famine had been experienced. Nevertheless, I stuck to it.

Day two was easier. I didn't feel hungry but was thirsty. As I discovered in hindsight, nearly a third of your daily water intake comes from food you eat, not what you drink. I chugged water down and got about my day as if everything was normal.

It wasn't until day three did I start to

experience any sort of physical effect. As I had not eaten, my blood sugar levels were low which is the biggest cause of headaches and migraines. While I did not have anything severe, I started to feel light-headed which continued until the end of the seventh day.

I will always remember the first meal I had at the end of that fast: sticky rice and mango pudding. The sweet mango mixed with coconut milk, sugar and salt, made delicious alongside glutinous rice. I will also remember the startling conclusion of the experiment: it wasn't too bad. I had practiced my worst fear, no food for a week, and only had a small headache to show for it. There is something incredibly empowering about that knowledge: That whatever happens, you'll be okay.

Note - Please don't try this yourself without seeking professional health advice and supervision.

The 3-30 Money Diet

After the fasting experiment I set about to discover the best way to save money. A method that had a similar level of shock and intensity but one that wasn't going to starve you. After rallying a small army of volunteers (thank you!) the results were compiled and developed into The 3-30 Money Diet.

It has been re-iterated, torn apart and put back

together in various forms but this is the final result proven to give the best results.

Since launch, The 3-30 Money Diet has shifted people out of relative poverty, empowered many to escape debt, rent traps and every other kind of money trouble. It's an adrenaline shot of money-saving steroids and will wake you up to what's possible with limited resources.

How it works

For three weeks you can only spend £30 (hence "*3-30*"). This is *after* accommodation, bills and commuting: Just day-to-day spending.

Sounds easy? Ha! We'll see, tough guy. £30 per week for all your food, coffees, snacks, impulse buys, shopping, drinks after work, dinner parties, taxies, wine, *everything*. Still think you can do all of that with £30?

Breakfast, lunch and dinner. Including the weekends. How much did you spend last night on dinner? Times that by seven. Now do the same for lunch and breakfast. *Hang on a minute, I've already gone over £30 just on dinner!*

The 3-30 Money Diet is a short and intense initiation into money saving. It's difficult but very rewarding. You'll wake up to how much things really cost, counting every penny in the supermarket, questioning even which supermarket you should go to and that's the whole point: Re-evaluate everything you spend money on. Become money conscious.

£30 per week, for three weeks.

What about afterwards? Start with that. Most money books are rarely stuck to because who's willing to go through hundreds of individual money saving tips? It's hard enough mustering the energy just to find out how much debt you have, yet alone paying it off.

Every money-saving tip, what-if and but-that is just another huge hurdle to climb: I don't want to use less toilet roll. I quite like my morning latte. But if you stick to one goal, one statistic, one target: £30 per week for 3 weeks, everything will fall in line. Trust me.

What do people say?

Justin from Colchester
"Holy mother of Jesus. When Tom first said about the £30 a week I thought what's the biggy? Then I thought about how I was going to do it. I planned what I thought were cheap meals for the week and went to my usual, Sainsbury's. I tallied it up and it came to £55. I had to go back round and put loads of stuff back, swapping to cheaper basic brands too. Eventually it got down. But then I had nothing else to spend. I went to work and came home every day without a wallet. I took packed lunch, cooked dinner and said no to the pub-after-work-crowd. But I saved so much money.

The second week I even had surplus. Tried Lidl which saved me a bomb - even got a bottle of wine - and managed to get my niece a little birthday present. The thing is, the money diet wasn't like a magical cure, it woke me up. I realised how much money I spend on stuff without even noticing. For years I've been sleep-spending. That's why it's really good."

Kejal from Lemington-Spa
"I found it such a challenge because I'm not very good at saying no to people. My friends always ask me out for dinner and stuff and I felt really uncomfortable saying no. When they asked why, I did what Tom said and just told the truth, that I was trying really hard to save money. They just accepted that and one friend even said what if she came over with some food and we made dinner together - that was surprising and made me realise it's not so bad. I guess what it taught me the most was how much money I was spending unconsciously. Like I wasn't in control because I kept saying yes to my friends on going out, shopping, dinners. Small things but they really add up."

Harry from Clapham, London
"The 3-30 Money Diet opened my eyes to a whole new world. I swapped supermarket which was a massive saver, invested £10 in my second week into fixing my bicycle which since then has saved me hundreds of pounds, and found a love for vouchers. I literally search for vouchers on everything before I buy now."

Sue from Chichester
"I managed to do The 3-30 Money Diet five times in a year. I took little breaks in between and did it again. Eventually I started feeling guilty when I wasn't doing it! Because it taught me how much I can live on if I actually try hard and plan ahead. Tom told me to get the kids involved and to make it a challenge for them. They could only get their usual treats if they found them for cheaper - they loved it. I've managed to pay off about £2,000 of debt."

What if you have a family?

The 3-30 Money Diet can be adapted to more than one family member. It's £30 per adult, and £10 per child. So if there are two adults and three children, spend only £90 a week for three weeks:

	Adults 1	Adults 2
Children 0	£30	£60
Children 1	£40	£70
Children 2	£50	£80
Children 3	£60	£90
Children 4	£70	£100
Children 5	£80	£110

Families have it toughest when it comes to

money-saving and debt clearance. There are some families of five I know who only have £40 a week to spend on food. This is definitely on the extreme end of the spectrum and I really respect them as incredible personal finance gurus. Having spent time with them in their homes, a few little pointers have been learnt will be of benefit to all:

- Buy big bags of frozen food. Frozen chicken, frozen fish, frozen vegetables and frozen fruit. They're much cheaper and can last.
- Always buy-one-get-one-free on non-perishable items. Stock up when you can and play the long-term game.
- Steer clear of cheap but low-nutrition foods such as chips and breaded fish. Banana and egg pancakes have loads of nutrition and are cheaper. When you do get money, try to fight the urge to buy *tastier* foods and stick to more *nutritious* foods.

Tools required

Technically you don't need anything to start and you should not spend much time dallying around waiting until you've got them before starting. Having said that, these may be useful:

- A cashbook for you to write down

everything you've spent money on (you can use a notes application on your phone)
- A separate current account for you to transfer £30 into at the beginning of the week, and then you only take that debit card out and about with you, OR,
- A cash card. You can get cash cards in some corner shops and the Post Office which allow you to top it up with £30 but then use it as a usual debit card when shopping. Alternatively, you could just take out £30 in cash and stick to it.
- Sign up to LatestDeals.co.uk for the best deals, discounts and voucher codes.

Other hints and tips
- Read the story of Justin from Colchester's experience on page 67. He found his usual supermarket was too expensive and swapped to a discount retailer, Lidl. Food is the biggest expense and it's well worth you taking a look at a cheaper brand: Lidl, Aldi, ASDA, Ice Land etc.
- Plan ahead. The most expensive way to eat is to shop on a daily basis. Buy food for the week and stick to the same meals that you rotate. This lets you buy in bulk, save money and not worry any more.

What else can I use The 3-30 Money Diet for?

Since creating The 3-30 Money Diet, people often tell me they use it for a variety of saving goals, not just to pay off debt. Usually it's to hit a savings target, for example in the run-up to a wedding, or for some other big expense.

I've also received plenty of feedback suggesting the experience can become a fun challenge between partners and friends. Who can cook the best meal on a budget? Who can save the most in a week? etc. etc.

The core purpose of The 3-30 Money Diet is to shock your system into recognising your spending habits which over the years have become invisible, even to yourself. It's to wake you up to how much you *really* spend and also for you to re-evaluate how much things need to cost. Sometimes because you've been spending X amount on a certain item for years, you assume that's the right price. Only when you see it for less, for example when it's on sale, do you consider perhaps it doesn't actually cost that much to make and the companies are just taking a profit margin. When you shop at a discount retailer the prices are cheaper not necessarily because the products are worse, but because the companies accept lower profit margins.

CHAPTER 7

Why you need to automate your money

Our human psychology is geared for the opposite of wise financial prudence. Daniel Kahneman, Nobel Prize Winner, wrote in his international bestseller, *Thinking, Fast and Slow*, of how we have two systems of thinking. With System 1, we think quickly and upon impulse. If we see something familiar, we are more inclined to like it. This is called the 'mere exposure effect'. The University of Michigan in America showed random Turkish words on the front of a student newspaper each week. Those that were shown more frequently were preferred (at the end of the year the researchers did a survey with the readers asking which of the random Turkish words they liked the most. A correlation was found between the words printed more frequently and those voted for the most). Advertisers take advantage of this by putting their brand name everywhere. Dior and Chanel, for example; you intrinsically like them - or at least think they have value simply because you've seen their name again and again.

Our System 1 mode of thinking is very susceptible to influence. When you read a story that makes you think of things that are old, aged, and slow, you are more likely to walk at a slower pace afterwards. This is called the 'Florida Effect', or the 'Ideometer Effect'. Our actions are easily influenced by ideas without us even knowing it.

System 2 thinking is conscious and deliberate. Mathematics, planning ahead and budgeting. When monitored through an MRI scanner, Kahneman found completely different parts of the brain are used when System 1 and System 2 are exercised.

System 1 'is the brain's fast, automatic, intuitive approach,' and System 2 is 'the mind's slower, analytical mode, where reason dominates.'

When we learn something new such as driving a car, we find it difficult and we have to concentrate. This is System 2 in action. With practice, we learn the movements and recognise patterns. Eventually, System 1 takes over and driving becomes intuitive. However, it takes a lot of practice to get to that point. This is where Malcolm Gladwell's idea of 10,000 hours comes from: it takes an average of 10,000 hours to master any skill.

Budgeting, paying bills, investing for the long-term; these are all System 2 processes. It isn't without lots of practice and will power that we can internalise them and make them System 1 modes of thought - intuitive, automatic and easy.

This is why most people don't like dealing with money problems. They're difficult, confusing and take much self-discipline (oh, and they're boring). There is a way to automate your finances so you only need to do them once. You can make your money manage itself: pay your bills, rent and mortgage, set a weekly budget and invest. You won't have to worry about self-discipline or will power.

CHAPTER 8

How to create your money system

Your money system needs to work for you. The core of it is a high-interest current account.

There are many different types of bank accounts and advice on how to save money gets complicated, fast. There's the current account which is bread and butter for most people, then there are savings accounts in which you earn interest on your money.

The pros and cons of each of these regularly change. *It depends* is the usual answer: how much you save, how much you earn, what the Government's set interest rate is etc. etc. *Money's Big Secret* would have to update itself every month to stay relevant.

To keep it simple there's only one thing you need to know when it comes to savings: the higher the interest rate, the better (remember, we're talking about savings not debt!). The bigger the percentage is, 1%, 2%, 5%, the more money you're earning on the back of your savings. For example, if you save £1,000 and earn 5% interest, you make £50 (which pays for a flight between London and Barcelona, for example).

Savings	Interest Rate	Interest Earned
£1,000	5%	£50
£5,000	5%	£250
£10,000	5%	£500

Where you get those high interest rates changes all the time. When setting up your banking infrastructure - how you're going to keep your money and spend it - you're going to need a bank account where you can receive money, keep, and spend it. You'll need a bank account that gives you a debit card, a bank account with online access so that you can pay bills and earn good interest on any savings you keep in it.

High-interest current accounts

You probably have a current account with a bank that doesn't pay you any interest at all. If you're unsure, look on the back of your card, call the number and ask.

You want to move your money to a current account that does pay interest. And yes, some current accounts are now paying interest. *Wait, I thought only savings accounts pay interest?*

At the time of writing, the UK economy isn't doing well and interest rates set by the Government are low. Savings accounts are offering low rates and customers aren't very interested in the paltry returns. Who wants to put away £1,000 for a year only to earn £10?

In a bid to attract new customers, banks are offering deals sometimes at a loss. High-interest current accounts are an example.

You create an account just like you would a normal bank account and you can use it in the same way. The benefit is that you get paid interest on any positive balance held at the end of the month. For example, at the time of writing in the UK, TSB offer a *Classic Plus* account which gives you 5% interest on £2,000.

So every year, if you hold £2,000 in your account, you will earn £100 interest. That pays for two flights from London to Barcelona, just for moving your money from one account to another.

What's more, in another bid to attract new customers, the same TSB *Classic Plus* account currently gives you 5% cashback on the first £100 you spend each month using contactless payments. Such benefits are increasingly common.

What do you mean by contactless payments? Modern debit cards and smartphones can now pay for items without using chip and pin. You just tap the card and. In the example above, TSB gives you 5% cashback on the first £100 you spend with this method, every month. So you can earn another £5 per month, or £60 per year, bringing the total *free* money you get up to £160 per year.

As you may have guessed, I use this account. However, there are plenty more. Some UK examples:

- Santander offers 3% interest on balances between £3,000 to £20,000
- Lloyds offers 4% interest on balances between £4,000 - £5,000
- Tesco Bank offers 3% on up to £3,000

Watch out for ripoff fees!

Banks make money from ripoff fees. A monthly fee for having an account, fees for overdrafts, fees for not putting in minimum monthly payments, fees for no reason whatsoever.

When looking for a new current account, watch out. Generally speaking, online only accounts such as First Direct behave, but still check the T&Cs.

The TSB *Classic Plus* account described doesn't have any monthly fees, gives you an optional overdraft (say no), and doesn't require you to put in a fixed amount every month. I like it for its simplicity. It's a loss-leading product for the company, which means they try to make money by selling you other stuff later on: mortgages, credit cards and loans. For as long as you say no to these - and there are ways to opt-out of their marketing - you'll simply be making free money.

How much should I keep in my current account?

You need to keep cash in your current account so you can pay your bills, rent and debt. On top of that, it's safe to have a cushion of cash in case of unexpected things: you lose your job, you get in an accident, you have a baby (one would hope you were expecting this!). I keep three months of living expenses in cash, which takes me to about the £2,000 mark.

Create a separate spending account

Money for daily spending (such as food and travel) you need to create a separate account for. Or, if you have moved your money from an existing account to a new high-interest current account, keep your original account open and use that for your daily spending. You're going to use this separate account for daily spending so that you can automatically budget yourself. This prevents you from ever going into debt and gives you the confidence of knowledge you're not over-spending.

Here's a clearer view of what you use each account for:

High-Interest Current Account	Normal Current Account
Debt repayments	
Cushion of cash	
Rent / Mortgage	Daily spending
Bills	
Investments	

How to automate your budgeting: direct debits and standing orders

Direct debits and standing orders are your main

tools when it comes to automated budgeting. Direct debits are when companies transfer money out of your account on agreed dates, usually to pay bills, and standing orders are instructions you give to your bank to pay someone a fixed amount on an agreed date.

The first and most important step is to ensure your income is being paid into your high-interest current account. Speak with your employer, change your bank account details, get it sorted. You can't pay bills out of an account you don't have money in.

Rent and mortgage repayments

Rent and mortgage repayments tend to be the biggest expenditures. Create a monthly standing order of the exact amount to be paid on the agreed date. For example, I have my rent paid by standing order on the first of every month.

Set this up and you'll never have to worry about paying your rent on time again.

Utilities and bills

Pay your utility bills by direct debit. Electricity, gas, water and council tax. It's nearly always cheaper to pay these via direct debit. If you're paying for these utilities when bills come through the letterbox (usually every three months), you could save £100s by switching to direct debit. Normally it's 6% cheaper than any other way of paying.

Furthermore, if you've never switched before, you could gain by switching to a cheaper tariff. Savings of £300+ a year are possible if you opt for a cheap tariff.

- Quick tip: Give your supplier regular meter readings and it'll give you a more accurate bill. If you don't, you may find you're paying for high estimates.

Mobile Phone Contract, Other Bills

Try to pay all your bills by direct debit. This is also a good opportunity to cancel some subscriptions. Do you really need your Netflix? Are you getting the most out of your gym membership? Are you listening to your Spotify music? Are there better things you can do other than watch Sky TV? My advice is to cancel them all and if you find yourself craving for them three months later, have a think about turning them back on.

By paying for everything via direct debit or standing order, you can calculate your exact monthly outgoings. For example:

- Rent: £650
- Gas & Electricity: £30
- Water: £15
- Council Tax: £65
- Internet & Line Rental: £15

- Mobile Phone: £30
- **Total: £805**

This is not an exact list and everyone will be different. Student debt, interest repayments on existing loans, car insurance, travel etc. add it all up.

As long as your income matches your outgoings, you know you can pay your bills and avoid going into debt. If you do The 3-30 Money Diet you will also be empowered with the knowledge that when push comes to shove you can survive on £30 a week for food. Any surplus can be invested and put towards gaining your future freedom and living a happy life.

Automated budgeting: Create your own money mentor

Automate your finances so that your bills are being paid with direct debits and standing orders and then you can now work out how much of your money you have left for budgeting and investing.

Again, this is where The 3-30 Money Diet comes into play. It's impossible for me to say or dictate how much money you need. It's also about your mindset. You may have a passion or interest that you receive much enjoyment from. For example, I enjoy a Brazilian martial art called *Capoeira* and spend £12 per week on classes. To others, this is a 'luxury'. To me, it's something I love. Everyone has their 'thing' and I believe life is too short not to do it. I can't exactly do a martial art when I'm sixty-five. Think back to Ben Sedan's olive trees and spend what you're able to on what you love. Ruthlessly cut back on *everything else*.

The 3-30 Money Diet will help you gauge how much you really need. There's no point in guessing because you always estimate more. Only when you force yourself to stick within a budget do you realise what you can make do with especially with some creativity.

If you have a family I recommend getting everyone involved. A technique that's worked time and again is to be honest with the children and to show them your shopping list. Tell them your total budget: £30, for example, and that you need their help to stick to it. Have them help you get the items on the list and tell them to look for the cheapest options. If there's any money left put it towards buying them a treat for their hard work.

Do The 3-30 Money Diet and find how much you really need on a weekly basis.

Then comes the genius part: Create a weekly standing order that transfers that amount of money from your high-interest current account to your spending account. This technique of automated budgeting will help you reign in the spending, stop your System 1 impulses and force you to keep on track. It's as if you have your own full-time personal finance mentor by your side.

How it looks altogether

STEP 1
Receive your income in your **high-interest current account**

STEP 2
Pay with direct debits and standing orders:
- Debt repayments
- Rent / mortgage
- Bills and utilities
- Travel and commuting

STEP 3
Budget a daily spend allowance (e.g. £30) and create a weekly standing order from your high-interest current account to your normal current account. Use this normal account for:
- Food
- Shopping
- Your Single Spending Allowance (SSA)

STEP 4
After leaving a cushion of cash (three months living expenses) invest the rest of your money automatically with a direct debit (Chapter 9).

Weekly versus monthly budgeting

If you get paid monthly you'll know what this is like: You receive a large amount of money at the end of the month and feel rich. *Woohoo, pay day!* Finally, you have money and you go to the pub or whatever it is and spend. By the end of the month you're back at zero impatiently waiting for the next pay day.

Had you ever printed out your transaction history, you will have noted a strong correlation between pay day and the amount you spend. Again, this is System 1 versus System 2 thinking. We're really bad at conscious, deliberate thinking but very good at making impulse decisions such as *ah, who cares, life's too short!*

You should set up a weekly standing order to help even out your spending account. This is because it reduces the peaks and troughs of your balance, and removes the psychological temptation to spend more money when you have it.

Create a weekly standing order from your high-interest current account to your spending account, for example, £30 per week. This way you won't have to spend time calculating how much you have for the rest of the month. You can see your balance and know that's it for this week. If you stick to it, you know you're within budget.

Why the poor don't buy more

I want to tell you a quick story that reveals more of our spending psychology.

When we earn more money, we spend more money, but we don't necessarily spend it on things that are good for us. We don't always pay off our debts, for example, nor buy more nutritious foods. This has been found across the world, even amongst the most poor.

Going back to Abhijit Banerjee and Esther Duffle's *Poor Economics*, the examination of how those on $1 per day live, they discovered a mind-blowing phenomenon. Contrary to what you'd expect, when you give malnourished people - those who are consuming significantly less calories than the recommended daily guideline - more money, they do not necessarily spend it on more food. While hunger and malnourishment is the first component of the poverty trap, 'The poor cannot afford to eat enough; this makes them less productive and keeps them poor,' when they're given money, studies show they don't always want to spent it on more food.

This sounds mad: The world's most hungry do not always buy more food when given money. Instead, 'among these very poor urban households, getting more calories was not a priority: getting better tasting ones was.'

People don't want *more* food, they want *better tasting* food. If you think about it, this is more natural.

'Households could easily get a lot more calories and other nutrients by spending less on expensive grains (like rice and wheat), sugar and processed foods, and more on leafy vegetables and course grains'. But as George Orwell noted in *The Road to Wigan Pier*, 'the point is, no human being would ever do such a thing. The ordinary human being would sooner starve than live on brown bread and raw carrots. And the peculiar evil is this, that the less money you have the less you are inclined to spend it on wholesome food...'

When we finally earn a bit of money, when we receive a big monthly pay packet, we're more likely to spend it on tastier things than more nutritious things. It's where our System 1 triumphs over System 2. In order to get rich we have to recognise and beat our own natural inclinations. The best way to do that is to create an automated money system which does it for us.

Pay off your debt automatically

Automate your money system to pay off as much of your debt as possible before you start investing. Begin with the most expensive debt. Refer back to the table of debts we made in Chapter 3 and automatically transfer as much as you can afford and a little bit more to paying it off.

If you've worked out your bills and switched to monthly direct debits, and if you've created a money system that automatically transfers a weekly spending allowance, everything (after leaving a little bit of cash in your high-interest current account for a cushion) should go towards paying off your debt.

Figure out the maximum you can pay back per month (always pay more than the minimum). If you divide the debt by that amount you can now work out approximately how long it will take before you're debt free. For example, if you have £5,000 of debt and you can pay back £350 per month (after interest repayments), you'll be debt free in 14 months. Obviously, the more money you can save and put towards your debt the faster you'll be free from it.

Visit tomchurch.co.uk/r/debt-calculator/ to work out exactly how long it will take you to pay off your debts.

Remember, that's the whole purpose of this book - to help you win back your freedom. You're an incredible individual who deserves to be able to live a life of choice. Not one spent paying someone else interest. I'll show you how to invest your money soon, but first you must pay off any expensive debt.

Say you had £1,000 of credit card debt at 17.9% interest (a standard rate). In the first year you'll pay £179 of interest.

Whereas if you invested £1,000 you may only earn 8% (see Chapter 9), £80. Therefore you're £99 better off (£179 - £80) putting your savings towards getting rid of your debt.

It's nearly always the case that debt costs more than what you can earn from investments and savings accounts, so generally speaking, pay off your debts before you invest or save. The two cases in which this may not be true are mortgages and student loans. Some mortgages will charge you an early repayment fee and if the interest rates are less than the average of 8% that you'll get by investing your money, you may not be better off. Student loans in the UK vary depending on when you went to university, how much you currently earn and how many years have passed since you took it.

- A quick pointer: If you've had your mortgage for over three years, you may benefit from re-negotiating your rates. This can save you £1000s over the term of the mortgage.

Case Study

Sean gets paid £1,400 per month after tax, national insurance and student loan repayments. His monthly outgoings are:

Income	**£1,400**
Rent	£-650
Gas & Electricity	£-30
Water	£-15
Council Tax	£-65
Internet & Line Rental	£-15
Mobile Phone	£-30
Travel	£-140
Remaining Balance	**£455**

When you deduct his monthly income of £1,400 by his monthly outgoings of £945, Sean has £455 left.

Sean does The 3-30 Money Diet, spending £30 per week on everything else, which is about £130 per month. This is for food, entertainment and all other purchases. And let me emphasise this point: The 3-30 Money Diet *is* doable. That leaves Sean with £325 per month.

Balance	**£455**
The 3-30 Money Diet	£-130
Remaining Balance	**£325**

He has a £2,000 credit card debt charging 17.9% interest. This is costing him £29.83 per month (£358 per year).

Sean puts the full £325 he has left over towards paying off his debt. Within seven months, he'll be debt free.

After paying off his debt, Sean releases the thrifty shackles and decides to enjoy few more 'luxuries'. However, he still wants to save and puts aside £250 per month for investment.

At 8% growth per year for 30 years, Sean's £250 per month will have grown to £372,589. He would have saved £90,000 himself and the other £282,589 will be the growth of his investment.

Monthly Saving	Interest Rate	Years	Total Return
£250	8%	30	£372,589

Enabling your money to grow is money's first big secret: it can grow faster and faster with time. Let me show you how it works.

CHAPTER 9

Why investment 'experts' are pointless

"When you think of investors who do you imagine?"

"Big shot dick-swinging Wolf of Wall Street pin-striped arseholes making billions by destroying the world."

James hates bankers. He takes an extreme-left view and says everything is pretty much, for lack of a better word, screwed. He's lived on farms, volunteered in communes, and considers himself the absolute opposite of profiteering investors.

However, he was surprised to learn - as you might be - that investors aren't very good at their jobs.

By investors, I mean the professional kind. Those that actively look after your money and try to grow it. Asset managers, stock picking managers, active managers, fund managers, mutual fund managers... They're all the same thing: people you pay to grow your money.

Most people think they don't know anything about the stock market or investing and so they should give their money to those that do. So you hand over all your savings to an 'expert' who promises you good returns for a fee. You give him or her your money, get your returns and think *good job, my money grew.*

Madison Marriage, a journalist for the

Financial Times, would like you to think again:

'Almost every actively managed equity fund in Europe... has failed to beat its benchmark over the past decade.'

Let me make that clear: nearly all professional investors in Europe failed to beat and deliver above market-average growth in the past 10 years.

'Overall in Europe, four out of five active equity funds failed to beat their benchmark over the past five years, rising to 86 per cent over the past decade, according to S&P's analysis of... 25,000 active funds.

'Within that sample, 98.9 per cent of US equity funds underperformed over the past 10 years, 97 per cent of emerging market funds and 97.8 per cent of global equity funds.'

Jeff Sommer of The New York Times reported similar results from America. 'How many mutual funds routinely rout the market? Zero'.

He said, 'The truth is that very few professional investors have actually managed to outperform the rising market consistently.'

'In fact, based on the updated findings and definitions of a particular study, it appears that no mutual fund managers have.'

Jeff looked at a study of 2,862 American actively managed funds and discovered only two managed to do better than the market average for over five years. Only two!

'If all the managers of the 2,862 funds hadn't bothered to try to pick stocks at all - if they had merely flipped coins - they would, as a group, probably have produced better numbers.'

Richard Evans of The Daily Telegraph reported for the UK, 'Just one fund manager in 100 beats the market'. The study, by the Pensions Institute at Cass Business School, found that 'actively managed funds returned an average of 1.4% less than the market'.

Only 1% of fund mangers managed to do better than tossing a coin.

Now, one reason for these bad results is because the managers have to pay themselves. So they make you money, let's say 10% growth, but deduct a 2% fee for doing so. This leaves you with 8% growth, which, in fact, is the US S&P 500 (an American stock index; see Chapter 10) market average over the last 50 years. You could have earned 8% yourself without trying nor any expensive fees.

Investors still get paid astronomical amounts of money despite being terrible at their jobs because of the huge sums involved. If their fund is £1 billion (which isn't very big in this industry) and they deliver 10% growth in a year: £100 million, and their fee is 2%, that's £20 million into their pocket.

You should not assume 'experts' can make you more money than you can do yourself.

Furthermore, and more importantly, if the 'experts' can't even beat the market average, you shouldn't try either.

Investors have huge teams dedicated to analysing everything under the sun. They try to make predictions and create complicated computer models of the future. If oil goes up, then this and that will happen. They spend hundreds of millions on this research and only rarely does it lead to superior results. The point is, if the 'experts' have all of this and you just have a laptop in your bedroom, how can you compete? You can't. Those who try are the ones who lose money.

You and I do not understand the market. We may think we do, but we don't. Even if we try, we will never be as equipped as the fund managers and our ability to sustain losses is nil. Fund managers can lose millions in a minute and not blink an eye. We don't even have millions to lose.

We need to stop trying to be experts ourselves, stop giving our money to experts who fail anyway, and invest our money directly into the market. How? With index funds.

CHAPTER 10

What are index funds?

After investors take their fees, almost none give you better than average market returns. But what does 'average market returns' actually mean?

Nearly every country has stock markets where companies sell equity to the public. You can buy and sell shares of these companies through these markets.

Stupid people buy and sell shares from individual companies. They buy £1,000 of Apple shares, for example, or Tesco, Vodafone, British Gas etc. I say stupid people because buying individual shares is inherently risky. Putting all your money into one basket is the fastest way to lose it.

Remember what we learned in the previous chapter? Even the 'experts' can't beat the market average. And if they can't choose winners with all their research teams and computer modeling then how can you?

Index funds are a combination of all the companies on a market. You will have heard of the FTSE 100. It's real name is the Financial Times Stock Exchange 100 and it has the 100 biggest UK companies listed on it: Barclays, Burberry, Coca-Cola, EasyJet, GlaxoSmithKline, Marks & Spencer, Next, Standard Chartered, Tesco, Unilever and many more.

When people say the 'market average', they

mean the average value of all these companies combined.

Every year EasyJet, Sainsbury's, Royal Mail and all the other companies try to grow. They all want to make more money. That growth increases their value or what's called their 'market capitalisation'. For example, their average value might be £1 billion this year, and £1.1 billion next year. That's an average growth of 10%.

By investing into an index fund, you're investing into the market average: all of the companies listed combined. When you put in £1,000, it gets divided between all the companies. You don't just invest into one company, you automatically invest into many.

This is why index funds are great. You put your money into one thing, the index fund, and it automatically diversifies it for you. Should one company do badly the risk of you losing money is minimised because you have divided it into many other companies too. Also, as index funds are automatic they charge very small fees, 0.2% is about average.

In one swoop you can invest your money into the UK's top 100 companies. More, in fact. There are hundreds of index funds for every market in every country. You can split your money across the world so not just UK companies but American, European, Japanese, 'emerging markets' and more.

You can put the cash you have in hand, the uncollected debt tokens, to work. By investing in the stock market you are getting the companies and banks to work for you. Technically, you own a bit of them. Hundreds of them!

I'm not alone in advocating such a simple approach. Warren Buffett, Chairman of Berkshire Hathaway, one of history's best performing funds, said in an interview, "The best way in my view is to just buy a low-cost index fund and to keep buying it regularly over time."

Peter Lynch an American investor who averaged a 29.2% annual return over his career said, "Most investors would be better off in an index fund."

Finally Burton Malkiel, economist and author of *A Walk Down Wall Street* wrote, 'Index funds have regularly produced rates of return exceeding those of active managers close to two percentage points.'

When I explained this to James, that he could have the bankers he detests so much to be working for him, his eyes lit up. He could invest his money automatically by setting up a direct debit into an index fund and sit back happy in the knowledge that it was automatically being diversified and would grow slowly over the long-term. People in suits sitting behind desks would be working hard to grow their companies and James would reap the benefit. It's the same principle as having your eggs in many baskets.

"How do I do it?" he asked.

CHAPTER 11

What does 2,000 years of history teach us about getting rich? Niall Ferguson, a renowned historian, sought the answer. In 2012 he published *The Ascent of Money: A Financial History of the World* which also became a popular TV show on Channel 4. Looking at how money as a currency evolved over time, from coin to note, stocks, shares and bonds, and what led to these changes (mostly war), he concludes that having looked at 2,000 years of history, the rise and falls of Kings, Queens, banking dynasties and Governments, the secret to getting and staying rich is to diversify your money.

It was always those who invested too much into too little that lost their wealth. Whether it was the Dutch Tulip mania in 1637 where single tulip bulbs sold for ten times the annual income of a skilled craftsman, or the French Mississippi Company in 1716 which generated such investor excitement that the national bank had to print more paper. Both examples crashed spectacularly with the latter leading to the French revolution. Millions of people lost their life savings because they got caught up in excitement listening to 'experts'. Had they diversified and invested their money into many companies and asset classes (I'll come on to that) they would not have lost their wealth.

Index funds are relatively new. They began in

theory in the 1950s when John Bogle from Princeton University wrote a thesis titled, 'Mutual Funds can make no claims to superiority over the Market Averages', and became practice in October 1970 when Qualidex Fund was incorporated as an index fund based on the top 30 companies of the Dow Jones (another American index).

The benefits of index funds have quickly become recognised. Even Warren Buffett said that the instructions on the estate he will leave for his wife is to put 90% into index funds.

As of 2014, index funds made up 20.2% of American stock market investments. This was double from 2007. In contrast, traditional actively managed funds have experienced people pulling money out. From 2007 to 2014, $659 billion less is being given to 'experts'. People are beginning to recognise that over the long-run, the fees investors charge are not worth it.

How to invest into an index fund

Getting set up and investing into an index fund will take a few hours over the course of the next week.

First you have to create an account with an online platform that facilities your investments. Here are some options for the UK:

- Hargreaves Lansdown (www.hl.co.uk)
- Fidelity (www.fidelity.co.uk)

- Nutmeg (www.nutmeg.com)

You'll need to give your personal details, bank account details as well as your national insurance number.

You'll also need to create a memorable username and password, sometimes even a second password. Make sure you have a secure method of remembering these because it can be a big pain if you forget.

The companies may review your request to create an account or may open one for you immediately. Usually they differ and sometimes you may get something in the post. So pay attention to how the sign-up process works but above all you should not be paying for anything. It's free to set up accounts with these guys.

If you want the most simple option, choose Nutmeg. It's incredibly easy to use. Just say how much you want to invest and for how long (remember, money's big secret is to play the long game, so if possible choose 30+ years). Then you must choose your level of risk. If you're investing over a long period of time you can afford a higher level of risk. If you're investing for a short period of time (10 years or less) choose a lower level of risk. Nutmeg will automatically choose index funds for you. Super easy.

If you want to take a slightly more active role, i.e. choosing which index fund you want to invest in, Hargreaves Lansdown and Fidelity are better. A little bit more complicated to set up an account but you get full control. While this is not an endorsement, I use Hargreaves Lansdown. To get rich you have to invest and to invest you have to open an account with an investment platform. Go ahead and do that now.

A word on ISAs

This bit is technical and you can always refer back to it later. Feel free to skip ahead to the next part, 'Should you seek dividends or growth?'

Investment savings allowances (ISAs) allow you to earn interest tax-free. At the time of writing, the UK Government gives an ISA of £15,240 per year. This means you can save £15,240 per year and whatever interest you earn on that is tax free.

However, there are different types of ISAs and the benefits are not the same.

First, there is the Cash ISA. This is where you put your cash into a savings account and earn interest. Again, at the time of writing you can put away £15,240 per year and whatever interest you earn will be tax free. This is great if you can find a savings account with high interest rates.

Secondly, there is the Stocks & Shares ISA. You buy stocks and shares (hopefully through an index fund) and there are two ways you can make money: either when you sell the stocks and shares at a higher value, or when you receive dividends. Dividends are a bit like interest on a savings account. If a company makes a profit, it gives some of it back to you; it could be on a regular basis or as a one-off.

The benefits of a Stocks & Shares ISA is different than a Cash ISA. This is because you already get some tax allowances for stocks and shares.

When you invest into stocks and shares, you already get a capital gains tax (CGT) allowance of £11,100. CGT is a tax you have to pay on the gain you make when selling things like shares, a second home and jewellery. However, you're allowed to make £11,100 of gains tax-free every year outside of an ISA.

So if you were selling your stocks and shares and it had grown in value up to but not more than £11,100 in one year, you would not pay any tax thanks to the CGT allowance. So you would only gain using a Stocks and Shares ISA in a year where you were making total gains over £11,100.

I mentioned there are two ways to make money from stocks and shares. Either when you sell them at a higher value, or receive dividends. When you receive dividends - a portion of the company's profits - you're taxed 10% in an ISA. So if you invest £15,240 in a single year, any dividends you receive shall be taxed at 10%. This is if you use the Stocks & Shares ISA.

However, and it's a big however, basic-rate taxpayers pay 10% on dividends anyway - even outside of an ISA. So if you earn up to £32,000 per year (the threshold of being a basic-rate taxpayer), you do not benefit from a Stocks &

Shares ISA in terms of reducing your tax on dividends as you're already benefitting from the lower tax rate. If you earn more than this, if you're a higher-rate taxpayer, outside of an ISA you have to pay 32.5% on dividends. Therefore, the Stocks & Shares ISA only helps higher-rate taxpayers in terms of reducing tax on dividends.

Will you benefit from using a Stocks & Shares ISA?

	Additional-rate taxpayer (45%)	Higher-rate taxpayer (40%)	Basic-rate taxpayer (20%)	Non-taxpayer
CGT < £11,100	✗	✗	✗	✗
CGT > £11,100	✓	✓	✓	✓
Tax on Dividends	✓	✓	✗	✗
Income Tax on Bonds	✓	✓	✓	✗

Should you seek dividends or growth?

Money's first big secret is to play the long-game. You want your money to grow over decades. When you're ready to take your money as an income, that's when you decide to receive dividends.

Dividends will be your future source of income. Companies share their profits with shareholders and the more shares you hold, the greater portion of profits you receive. Until then - until you're ready to retire or take your income - you want to grow your shareholding as much as possible.

When deciding whether or not to use a Stocks & Shares ISA, don't get bogged down in the details. It's better just to do it than not. You can also open a Cash ISA and both are free to do. Over the long-term stocks and shares have historically always outgrown the returns of interest from savings accounts (however, as always, it's pertinent and a legal necessity to say that past results are not a guarantee for the future: remember, investments can go down as well as up).

Using an ISA is free to do and you only stand to gain. As we're interested in growing our money over the long-term, the Stocks & Shares ISA is more relevant to us and we'll be putting more money into it than the Cash ISA. We'll also be seeking growth over dividends until we're ready to retire or take our money out.

How to open a Stocks & Shares ISA

Create your account with the investment platform such as Hargreaves Lansdown and you'll find right on the homepage a button to open a Stocks & Shares ISA. Give your personal details and your National Insurance number again. They may ask how you'd like to add money to your ISA, whether it's a single lump sum or regular monthly savings. Choose regular monthly savings. A few other questions and you're done!

How to choose an index fund

If you're using Nutmeg, they will chose various index funds for you. Simply say how much you want to invest - do as much as you can - and set a risk level (but remember, always pay off expensive debt first). I'm investing over a 35 year period and have set my investment level to eight.

Nutmeg will then show you the portfolio it will create for you: how it will split your money and invest it into many different things. Remember Niall Ferguson's conclusion of studying 2,000 years of history: the secret to growing and keeping your wealth is to diversify. Nutmeg does this for you, automatically. It shows you exactly where your money is going in a clear and simple to use dashboard.

There are many index funds from many

different countries in many different markets. You want to spread your money across all of them. At the time of writing, at risk level 8, Nutmeg will invest your money into:

- Vanguard FTSE 100
- Vanguard S&P 500
- UBS MSCI EMU 100% hedged to GBP UCITS
- UBS ETF MSCI Japan 100% hedged to GBP UCITS ETF
- and many more

What do these mean?

Ugly names for simple things. Your money will go into the FTSE 100 which is the top 100 UK companies; the S&P 500 which is the top 500 US companies; the MSCI EMU which is the top 230 companies in 11 european countries; the MSCI Japan which is a collection of the top Japanese companies.

There are many more index funds Nutmeg will automatically invest your money into as well. More American companies, Indonesian companies, European companies and Japanese companies. Some big, some small, some fast.

As well as all of this, your money is also invested into 'safer' index funds too such as Government bonds.

What are Government bonds?

You lend your money to the Government and it promises to pay you back with interest. You can then sell this bond to other people. There are whole markets trading in these bonds, which as they're the Government, people consider safer. After all, it's much harder for a Government to go bust than it is for a company. So Nutmeg will invest some of your money into these Government bond markets as well. Not only do you now have the world's largest companies working for you, you also have Governments too!

A quick note on Nutmeg

- In order to invest with Nutmeg you must be able to put in an initial £500, then a minimum of £100 per month until you reach a total of £5,000.
- Nutmeg charges a fee of between 0.3%-0.95% per year which is still way less than usual fund managers, but not as cheap as if you were to do it yourself.
- However, there is a benefit to having a company automatically invest your money for you every month. You can literally set and forget. It's the ideal money system for those who want the simplest option.

How to do it yourself

If you're not using Nutmeg and have chosen something like Hargreaves Lansdown or Fidelity, you can do the job of Nutmeg yourself very easily and for lower fees.

You don't need to choose individual funds such as the FTSE 100 or the S&P 500, rather you can invest into a fund that'll split your money into many funds just as Nutmeg does.

Examples of this are the Vanguard LifeStrategy funds. You put your money in and they split it up across many index funds. Similarly to Nutmeg you can also choose your risk.

If you search for 'Vanguard LifeStrategy' on Hargreaves Lansdown, you'll see there are number of options differing by the percentage of equity they hold. For example:

- Vanguard LifeStrategy 20% Equity
- Vanguard LifeStrategy 40% Equity
- Vanguard LifeStrategy 80% Equity
- Vanguard LifeStrategy 100% Equity

You should think of this percentage as a level of risk. 20% equity is level two risk. 100% equity is level 10 risk. Again, the longer your investment horizon the more risk you should take.

What happens is when you invest your money into, say, the 40% equity fund, it'll put 60% of your money into the 'safer' bets such as Government bonds, and just 40% into companies. In the same way as I choose level eight on Nutmeg for my risk level, I choose 80% equity for the Vanguard LifeStrategy.

To invest with Hargreaves Lansdown, once you've created your account and opened a Stocks & Shares ISA, go to 'My Accounts' and you'll see 'Stocks & Shares ISA' there. Click it and you can now invest into it.

However, we're not just interested in a one time investment, we want to set up an automated money system where every month you invest your savings. Using Hargreaves Lansdown as the example because that's the one I use, open your Stocks & Shares ISA account and go to 'Monthly Savings'. From there you can add a fund. Look for the one you want to invest in and type in the monthly amount.

Make sure you've worked out how much you can afford to invest. Your household bills and expenditures should be paid by direct debit and you should have your high-interest current account to which you automatically pay in a weekly spending allowance and leaving a cushion of cash - ideally three months. Any remaining income can be invested. Whatever that is, enter it as the monthly savings for your investments.

Find the fund you'd like to invest in, choose what level of risk you're comfortable with and make sure you choose an 'accumulation' fund rather than 'income'. Set the monthly investment amount and you're done! You have created a fully automated money system.

What's the difference between an accumulation and income fund?

Some funds say they're 'Income' and others say they're 'Accumulation'. What does this mean? If you chose 'income', the money earned from any dividends will be paid to you in cash. It'll sit in your account until you either withdraw it or manually re-invest it. If you choose 'accumulation', the money will automatically be re-invested. As we want our money to grow as much as possible over the long-term, we're interested in 'accumulation funds'. It's just another automatic money system that helps us.

Three golden rules to remember

1. The value of your investments can go down as well as up, so you could get back less than you invest.
2. This book aims to provide information to help you make your own informed decisions. It does not provide personal advice based on your circumstances.
3. If you are unsure of how suitable an investment is for you, please seek personal advice from a qualified Financial Advisor.

With those legal wiggles said, let's have a look at where your money will go.

If you invest in the 'Vanguard LifeStrategy 80% Equity Accumulation' fund, your money will be split across many things:

- Top UK companies
- Top US companies
- Top European companies
- Top companies in all developed countries
- Top Japanese companies
- Top companies in emerging markets
- Global Government bond markets
- UK Government bond market
- and more.

It'll be automatically divided across many sectors too:

- Bonds
- Banks
- Pharmaceuticals & Biotechnology
- Oil & Gas Producers
- Software & Computer Services
- Technology Hardware & Equipment
- General Retailers
- Financial Services

- Travel & Leisure
- Media

Your money will be well and truly diversified. That's not to say you can't lose money, you can - a global financial crisis effects everything and everyone - but you'll be safer against small individual crises such as a single company going bust.

1% fee, 20% less money

Every fund charges a fee. This is a percentage of the income or growth you've gained. It's very, very, very important to pay attention to fees.

Fund managers compete with each other on fees: it's how they make their money. And novice investors don't pay enough attention to them. They see a 1% fee and think *wow, that's cheap, no worries*. They are so stupidly wrong. Here's why:

Pat started investing when she was 25 years old. She saved and invested £500 per month for 30 years (until she was 55). *Good job!* Her money grew at 7% per year and she accrued £609,985.50. *Awesome.*

Chris also started investing when he was 25 years old. He saved and invested the same amount, £500 per month for 30 years (until he too was 55). *Good job!* His money grew at the same 7% per year, **but, and it's a big but**, he was charged a 1% management fee. After 30 years, the same amount of time as Pat, he accrued only £502,257.52.

That's £107,727.98 (17.7%) less than Pat. All because of a 1% management fee!

So in case this isn't clear: look at the management fees.

Index funds are great because they are typically very cheap. Less than 1%. However, there are differences among them and it pays to shop around.

Nutmeg charges 0.95% but do-it-yourself Vanguard LifeStrategy 80% Equity charges 0.24%. Saving £500 per month for 30 years, assuming 7% annual growth, you'd be £74,783.57 better off with Vanguard. It's a tiny management fee difference but it has a huge knock-on effect. What's more, the greater amount your money grows, the more you'll lose to management fees.

Note - Nutmeg says it'll reduce its management fee as you invest more money so the example above may not be an accurate forecast. Rather, it serves to show the impact of a 0.71% management fee difference.

Your automated money system

When you have your money system set up, it's pretty cool. Your life satisfaction grows exponentially. Here are three key benefits:

1. You remove the stress of paying bills.

Direct debits take care of paperwork and you save hundreds of hours over your lifetime. You never have to worry about whether you've missed a payment, you never run the risk of being fined, and by being on direct debit you tend to get a cheaper rate helping you save more money as well.

2. No more anxiety or worry about money. Turning all your expenses into exact and predictable monthly amounts means you know precisely where you stand. You know how much money you need to make and for as long as you meet that target you're good to go. Life satisfaction increases by a magnitude of 10 times or more when you're not up at night worrying about whether you'll be able to pay next month's rent. By working towards a cushion of cash - three months living costs - you know you'll be alright.

3. Freedom from future fear. Ask any of my friends and they'll tell you how in the past fear of the future, retirement and old age would stress me. I worried about how I was going to live for I couldn't afford a house, nor a pension and wasn't saving much either. With your automated investments you know your future is in a much better place. Just remember that for every £1 invested now, in 30 years at 8%, it'll be worth £10. Yep, that impulse trip to

the pub now could be a week's worth of food in the future.

CHAPTER 12

How rich will you be?

Throughout this book I have usually used a predicted average growth figure of 8% per year. This is based on the last fifty years of the S&P 500 market (American top companies). I did this to keep it simple. However, now you know about index funds you will have noted that your money won't just be in a single market, it'll be in many, each with their own rates of return. It'd be more prudent then to think of your growth rate as a range, for example, between 4% - 9%.

The Vanguard LifeStrategy 80% Equity fund, for instance, has grown an average of 7.75% since its inception in 1994. However, within that there have been astonishing years such as 16.96% growth in 2012 and 17.52% in 2014, as well as bad years such as 4.93% and -1.86%.

It's best to give yourself a probabilistic range such as 4% - 9% but to make the mathematics a bit simpler you could just take the middle number of 6%. It's slightly conservative which is a good thing.

Also note the factor of inflation. Money's second big secret is that it was actually invented as a measurement of debt; the cash you hold is an unclaimed promise. By investing your money you put that promise to work. Companies and governments around the world work to grow your money and to return value to you. Then, when you're ready to retire you can sell your shares or switch to an 'income fund' (remember the difference between accumulation and income funds?) which will pay you dividends. However, when you do receive money for your shares in the long-term future, you'll be holding cash again. This cash won't be as valuable as it is today because of inflation. Prices will have increased and the money won't go as far. Since 1986, Britain has experienced an average inflation rate of 2.7%. This means prices of household goods have increased that amount every year.

Yet, there are some interesting quirks about the way inflation is measured in Britain. Firstly, the Government does *not* include the price of buying a home. Renting is included but house prices are not. The motives behind this are unclear but seeing as though buying a house may be your single biggest purchase, it does seem odd that it's not included. Make note - house prices have grown faster than inflation for over thirty years.

The second quirk about how inflation is measured is the basket of goods the Government chooses to measure the price of. It includes: Games consoles and online subscriptions, e-cigarettes, protein powder, sweet potato, headphones, craft beer and mobile phone accessories. The Government tries to create a picture of the average British person to come up with a single figure. However, everyone is different and you might not buy e-cigarettes or sweet potatoes. In fact, your personal inflation rate may be very different than the Government figure.

Inflation is measured by creating a 'basket of goods' with different categories of spending given different weightings. For example, in 2015 the Office for National Statistics, the Government body in charge of measuring inflation, assigned transport a 14.9% weighting and said its observed variation in price was 'medium'. If you work from home, or when you retire and don't work any more, it's likely that you won't be travelling within the country as much. Therefore, this inflation measurement does not apply to you. Similarly, you may not go to hotels and restaurants often which are given a 12.1% weighting. Instead, perhaps you spend more of your money on recreation and culture which is given a 14.7% weighting.

Your inflation figure will be different than the national average of 2.7%. Yet, the main point is that prices tend to go up which eats into your growth.

If your money grows at 8% per year but inflation is 2.7%, then in *real* terms, your money has only grown by 5.3% each year. The table below shows how much money you could expect to have, adjusted for inflation. That means in *today's* value.

Investment table adjusted for inflation

Per month	£100	£300	£500	£1,000
10 years	£13,969	£41,910	£69,842	£139,700
20 years	£34,345	£103,037	£171,729	£343,459
30 years	£66,360	£199,081	£331,801	£663,602
40 years	£118,696	£356,090	£593,485	£1,186,970

To be clear, the previous table shows numbers in *today's* value. £10 today is not worth the same as £10 in 40 years. The numbers have been adjusted for inflation. So the table gives you a clearer picture of how much your money will be worth in terms of prices today.

Inflation takes a huge chunk out of your future money's growth. The following table shows how much your money grows *without* adjustment for inflation. These are the figures your money could actually grow to, but remember, £10 today is not the same as £10 in forty years' time. Again, it assumes an 8% average annual growth rate.

Investment table *not* adjusted for inflation

Per month	£100	£300	£500	£1,000
10 years	£18,295	£54,884	£91,473	£182,946
20 years	£58,902	£176,706	£294,510	£589,020
30 years	£149,036	£447,108	£745,180	£1,490,359
40 years	£349,101	£1,047,302	£1,745,504	£3,491,008

Calculating your future income

The table above shows how your money can grow faster and faster with time and that it pays to start early. Now imagine you're 40 years into the future and you've finished growing your money: time to retire, accept your wrinkles and travel the world. You don't just eat into your savings pot until it runs dry, you can take an income from it.

Once you've finished growing your money you'll switch from accumulation funds to income funds. These focus on companies that pay dividends. Rather than re-investing money to get more growth, you take that money as cash.

Top UK companies pay an average dividend of 5% per year. Some more, some less. So if you have a total savings pot of £300,000, you can earn £15,000 from it every year. That's 5% of your total savings.

Most people when they retire do a combination of receiving dividends and eating into their savings.

To calculate your future income, take your predicted total savings figure adjusted for inflation and multiply it by 5% (0.05). This is what you can expect to receive every year from interest and without eating into the total savings pot. Again, it's better to use a probabilistic range, say between 3% - 7% but to keep it simple 5% is a good expectation.

How to beat inflation

You will have noted just how much inflation eats into your moneys' growth by comparing the two previous tables. If you save £300 per month for 40 years, you're over £600,000 better off if there was no inflation!

I wrote at the beginning of this chapter that inflation rates are calculated by the Government and not set in stone. Everybody is different: it depends upon what you buy. Therefore, your inflation rate may not be 2.7%, it may be 10% or it may be 1%.

However, there are ways you can get rid of the effects of inflation entirely, or perhaps even make it a negative figure. In other words, you can live more cheaply than you do today.

The single best way to achieve this is to move abroad. This is why so many retired British people move to Spain, Portugal and elsewhere. Prices are cheaper and money goes further. My parents retired to Malaysia where the cost of living was seven times cheaper. Whereas in the UK they would have had an average quality of life, in the Far East they could enjoy all kinds of luxuries.

Traditionally, buying a house was the second best way to make your money go further when you're older. By the time you retired it was expected that you would have paid off your mortgage and therefore had no more debt or rent to pay. The income you received from your investments was purely for spending. These days however, if you're not a homeowner this tactic is gone. House prices are too expensive. Yet don't despair if this is you. Note that you're able to invest the money you would have spent on higher mortgage repayments and house repairs. Renting comes with the benefits of not paying for house insurance, boiler repairs, decorating costs and more. All that money can go into your investments.

Another method to beat inflation is to keep the amount you spend each year the same. Using an automated money system, if you budgeted yourself the same spending amount every week and stuck to it, you'd be beating inflation. This may get tricky however, as if a sweet potato today was £1, and the Government is correct in assuming it'll increase in price by 2.7% every year, in 40 years time it'll cost £2.90. You may not be able to get very much food for the same amount of money.

A better method of beating inflation each year is to do what I call an *inflation reset*. There are two ways I do this: The first is with The 3-30 Money Diet. I do it twice a year which based on my own spending habits means I save 8% on what I would have normally spent each year. This more than negates the effects of inflation. In fact, doing it just once would be suffice. The second inflation reset tactic is to move abroad for a few months of the year. In some online circles this is called a mini-retirement. For example, if you moved to Spain for three months where the cost of living is 15% cheaper at the time of writing, assuming the cost of the flight wasn't astronomical, you'd also smash the effects of inflation. It's from Madrid, right now, that I write this.

Follow me on Instagram and Facebook to learn more about inflation resets, mini-retirements and traveling abroad:
- tomchurch.co.uk/r/instagram
- tomchurch.co.uk/r/facebook

Future technologies will make our lives cheaper

In the coming years there are two technological changes that will make our current living standards much cheaper: robotics and the internet of things.

Car manufacturers can now produce an electric vehicle from start to finish within a day. From a single sheet of metal they can bend, cut and weld an entire car together and if you've ever been to or watched a video of a factory it's an incredible, awe-inspiring sight. Robots do most of the work and it's mesmerising. Fewer and fewer people are needed to produce the products we enjoy, whether it's cars, phones or shoes. Apple, for instance, is working on robots to produce the iPhone removing the need for vast factories in China. Automation of production means the costs of making these things will go down. In turn, this will lead to lower prices for us.

The internet of things refers to the ever-increasing amount of information collected and connected. Cars and lorries will drive themselves and be able to talk to each other allowing for faster and cheaper transport. I'm good friends with Alex Shlagman, the best-dressed technology entrepreneur in London, who has spent years connecting the inventories of small independent shops and putting them on the internet. This means you'll soon be able to search for an item and it'll show you the cheapest place to get it in the country. The information will also show you the closest place you can get it. Furthermore, connect that data with an automated logistics service and you can get it driven to your door almost for free. His company is called Pocket High Street.

These technological advancements mean certain things will become cheaper although there are also concerns. For instance, what happens to all those people who lose their jobs?

CHAPTER 13

What should you do when the next financial crisis hits?

Every so often a financial crisis hits and the world economy plunges into an abyss. Headlines rock the Earth and red lines zig zag across charts pointing downwards. Experts declare the apocalypse has arrived and you should sell everything while you can.
Ah, experts.

Booms and busts are part of the economic cycle. If the economy has been going well for a while people start to forget the last recession and invest with ever more confidence and ignorance. Eventually, like the experts who become over-confident in their own predictions, investors tend to over-value things. When the rug is pulled out from under their feet they shriek as the real floor they have been standing on is revealed. Prices fall back to where they should have been and sometimes further as people then undervalue businesses out of fear.

Money's first big secret is that it can grow faster and faster with time. The longer your investment horizon is the less you need to worry about booms and busts. Over a 40-year period a recession is just a blip. You may not even see it on a graph.

The money system explained in this book has a

built-in mechanism to deal with booms and busts: it's called dollar cost averaging (DCA).

By investing the same amount every month automatically, you spread your risk. If markets are low (for example, during a recession), your money buys more equity. If markets are high (for example, during a boom), your money buys less equity. It automatically adjusts so that you buy more when things are discounted and less when they're expensive.

Possibly the worst thing you could do during a recession or financial crisis is pull your money out. It depends on a few things, of course, but really you should ignore the headlines and keep investing. You'll buy more equity for the same amount of money so that in the long-term you'll earn more when you come to sell or change to receiving dividends. It's difficult to turn a blind eye to the biggest media organisations all shouting about doomsday but that's what you have to do.

Remember to always seek professional financial advice before making any decisions. Your investments can go up as well as down.

When is it too late to start?

The tables in Chapter 12 show it's never too late to start saving and investing. However, if you want to make a decent living then the longer you wait the more you'll have to save each month.

Starting young makes things much easier but if you're older it's not impossible.

If you're 35 or older, it's more likely that you'll have a higher paying job than a younger person, already have savings and be in a more secure housing situation. Use the tables in Chapter 12 to work out approximately how much you'll need to save and invest in order to hit your financial goals.

There is a blogger online I have great respect for who goes by the name of 'Weenie' (quietlysaving.co.uk). She started saving and investing towards her pension when she turned 40 and every month reveals her figures. Brilliant and refreshingly transparent, she's an inspiration to how it's never too late to start and indeed has achieved great amounts in just a few years.

Furthermore, if you've worked for a company for many years it's likely that you've received pension contributions. Research what these are and remember they too go towards your savings and investment goal.

Renting versus buying: the false logic

Young people in Britain face a great hurdle at present when it comes to buying a house. They have been priced out of the market and the dream of owning their own home is gone. Unless the housing market collapses - unlikely to happen because of how much Britain's banks rely upon mortgage lending- the problem is unlikely to be fixed in our lifespan. Even if huge new house building initiatives were announced it would be decades before they are completed. I spoke with an engineer who works with Urban & Civic, a firm constructing a new town of 40,000 new homes outside Cambridge, and he explained it will take up to 20 years to finish. Shelter, a housing charity, says Britain needs 10 times that amount of housing to be built every year. Britain's housing crisis is here to stay and young people need to adapt.

There are saving and investment opportunities that come with not investing in a home. Many people don't realise how expensive owning a home is and most importantly that it's still a significant investment risk. Owning a home is no different than owning equity in a company in the sense that its value can go up and down due to circumstances outside of your control. If the housing market in Britain does fall, millions of homeowners will be stuck with debts far larger than the assets they hold. In other words, you'll only be able to sell your home for less than what you paid for it, leaving you with a big hangover of mortgage debt. Of course, the answer is not to sell and just to wait in the same way as when there's a financial crisis.

Furthermore, pouring so much money into one asset, a building, is inherently risky. *Money's Big Secret* has advocated a low-risk approach to investing: diversify your money across hundreds of companies and Government bonds in many different countries. If one goes down, you'll be fine. Investing in a house is the opposite approach: all your money in one basket. You can't rely on it to grow consistently over 40 years and neither will it give you an income to live on until you rent it out (in which case you'll either have to buy another home or rent). No, buying a home is not the be all and end all. If you are unable to get on board this market you're right to recognise others have been lucky, but leave it at that and do not despair.

With the money you would have paid to the bank through an expensive mortgage, you can instead save and invest it. You're free from location to chase higher paid work or to travel and are not tied down in the same way. Embrace it and maximise the opportunities available.

What target should you aim for?

How much should you save and invest and for how long? What target should you aim for?

Perhaps you want to live an extravagant lifestyle and enjoy the luxuries on offer. Perhaps you want to help the less fortunate and create a wealth fund that'll support your philanthropic efforts. Perhaps you want to retire into your reading chair and open *Lady Chatterley's Lover*. To decide your financial target you need to define your ideal lifestyle and divide the cost into a monthly figure. Keep in mind doing and experiencing things is cheaper than owning things and factor inflation with your estimates. You can use that figure as a rough figure but I tend to encourage a simpler philosophy: save and invest as much as you can and work towards increasing that amount every month.

The most important step to growing your money is to start today. Not when you get your next pay rise, not when you come back from holiday, not when the children have finished school. You have to start today with what you've got. Save where you can, pay off your expensive debts, and put whatever you have into index funds. Every month try to save and invest a little bit more. If you do your best, you'll be great.

Use the tables in Chapter 12 to work out how much you need to invest every month and for how long in order to reach your target.

Conclusion

The idea for Money's Big Secret came from reading a book about oak trees. Like it, The Man Who Planted Trees, I wanted to write a classic that would stand the test of time. There are hundreds of books giving you tips and tricks, strategies upon strategies and complicated methods but few which simply share the basics: if you plant a hundred acorns a day, you will grow a mighty oak forest.

None of the books I read considered what money actually is, nor thought about how it's different for everyone. Money is a very social thing just like a cup of tea and when you peel through the wild assumptions of economists and look at the evidence, you discover it wasn't even created for exchange but as a measurement of debt. We all owe each other but there's nothing solid underneath it. Money is just what we believe it to be and if one day we all woke up and said, "You know what? I'm not interested in this money thing anymore" the whole system would collapse. However, that's not to say that's what we want.

The financial system enables money to grow faster and faster with time. Companies are organised in such a way that they chase growth all day, every day. You can use this to your advantage by investing in them, whether it's £1 or £1 million. By understanding how money grows you also learn how the richest people in the world keep getting richer and why inequality grows at an ever faster pace.

Reading history reveals that the secret of keeping your wealth over time is to diversify, diversify, diversify. Buying individual stocks and shares, or putting all your money into a house is full of risk. What if that company goes bust? What if your house catches fire? What if people realise gold is just a yellow-coloured metal? I've shared the simplest way to invest your money across all markets and asset classes in many countries, and also for the cheapest fees. I've shown you how to beat inflation and the most important thing of all: to start early.

Debt is something you need to get much more comfortable with in the sense of understanding how much it's costing you. For every £10 you're spending on interest repayments now, you're losing out on £100 in 40-years time with 8% year-on-year growth. Pay it off as soon as you can with The 3-30 Money Diet and by lowering your interest rates, then start putting that money towards your investments.

Taking the first step requires will power, courage and determination. I've shown how you can automate your finances and create a money system that works for you. Just by setting up a high-interest current account along with your regular current account you can use standing orders and direct debits to automatically pay your debts, rent, bills, travel as well as budget your weekly spend. The rest (after saving a cushion of cash) can go towards your investments, which again is automatic and fully diversified following the same principles that have kept the rich wealthy for over 2,000 years.

Once you've successfully set up your money system, the next questions are: how can you make it go further? How can you live a better life on a smaller income? And how can you earn more money with less time?

Discover these answers by following me on my blog, **tomchurch.co.uk/blog**, and by joining my new venture, LatestDeals.co.uk (I explain more in the Afterword).

Thank you for reading Money's Big Secret, I hope you've enjoyed it.

If you have any questions you can get in touch with me on Facebook or Twitter:
- tomchurch.co.uk/r/facebook
- twitter.com/tomchurch

* * * * *

Review this book on Amazon

What topic have you enjoyed the most? Would you be so kind as to leave a generous review on Amazon to help spread the word?

Reviews help others discover the book and hopefully they'll learn something too.

Either way, thank you again for your time and for reading Money's Big Secret.

Tom

* * * * *

AFTERWORD

When reading a book about money it's easy to become obsessed with money itself. How much more you need to earn, how much things cost and how much you're investing. Yet my intention with Money's Big Secret is not to turn you into a number crunching Grinch. In fact, I want you to focus on the opposite: life and fun. By focusing on automation and creating a money system that does everything for you, the aim is that you don't have to think about money at all. Everything happens behind the scenes and you can go back to drinking tea with friends.

However, the conclusion you'll most likely arrive at having read the book (as I did having researched and written it) is you need to save and invest more money. When I first started, I set myself the target of investing £500 per month. This was more than double what I was doing already and that money had to come from cutting back on my daily spend.

Only when I began to discover the world of money bloggers, discount codes and deal forums did I learn how to achieve the same standard of living with less money. In fact, I began to live an even better standard of living.

It is a whole new world and discovering it is my next adventure. After writing this book, Deepak Tailor of LatestFreeStuff.co.uk and I decided to start a business together. It's called

LatestDeals.co.uk and we gather the best deals, discounts and voucher codes into one place and reward you for sharing them. The goal is to create a tool to help people save and make money. It's fantastic. Join in the adventure by visiting the website or downloading the app.

Books referenced in Money's Big Secret can be found on my blog, along with more resources, tools and reading lists: tomchurch.co.uk/blog

Printed in Great Britain
by Amazon